THE PURSUIT OF MEANING

THE
PURSUIT OF MEANING

Logotherapy Applied to Life

JOSEPH B. FABRY

BEACON PRESS

BOSTON

*To Judy who taught me the meaning
of being a husband; to Wendy, Claire, and
Richard who showed me the meaning of fatherhood;
and to Max who demonstrated the meaning of friendship.*

PREFACE

In this book Dr. Fabry has set himself a threefold goal: to popularize logotherapy — without vulgarizing it; to simplify its theories — without oversimplifying them; and to "Americanize" logotherapy — by focusing on those of its aspects that speak to readers brought up in the cultural climate of present-day America. To this end, Dr. Fabry had to skip what is too deeply rooted in the specifically European tradition of psychiatry and philosophy.

I must confess that this approach implies some sacrifice on my part. It was no less a great mind than Albert Einstein who once said that for the scientist there is one choice only: either to write in a profound and unintelligible way or else to write in an intelligible but superficial manner. While I would not want to claim that my academic writing should be classified as unintelligible, yet in this age of division of labor I feel that I should leave it to Dr. Fabry to write on logotherapy in a manner directed toward the layman, even at the risk of sacrificing some scientific precision. Nevertheless, Dr. Fabry's fresh and anecdotal style suggests a dilemma which we both tried our best to avoid. The casual reader still may sometimes find it difficult to discern exactly who says what: is Fabry quoting Frankl, or is he interpreting Frankl, or is he expressing his own thoughts? Although I have given Dr. Fabry all the assistance he asked for in preparing the manuscript, he was left completely free in interpreting logotherapy, in extrapolating its basic assumptions, and — to use the words of the book's subtitle — in "applying it to life." Logotherapy is not a closed system; any attempt to advance and develop it is invited and welcomed.

Thanks to both the author and the publisher, a comprehensive bibliography of logotherapy has been included, listing the American literature and also some of my German works from which Dr. Fabry drew information. Thus, one may expect that the book will be of service to the specialists as well as to the general public. To the specialists the primary sources on logotherapy, my own writings, are available. To take up their study will be mandatory at least for those who wish to polemicize against my teachings.

For the general public, Dr. Fabry's book provides excellent material that illustrates the individual tenets of logotherapy, and does it in a language that avoids abstract and technical terms. This is in accord with the principles of logotherapy. As my oldest cofighter, Paul Polak, once put it, "Logotherapy translates the self-understanding of the man in the street into scientific language." If this be true, I would say why not help the man in the street to cope better with everyday life by retranslating logotherapy into his own language? Whatever I am teaching — I have learned it from my patients in the first place. Therefore it is only fitting to repay them — by preventing others from ever becoming patients at all.

I am convinced that Dr. Fabry's book performs a needed service by spreading the message of logotherapy so that more people may profit from it. If it is true, as some truly great men have stated, that logotherapy "speaks to the needs of the hour," then Dr. Fabry should surely be rewarded by the impact and influence his book will have on the thinking and the lives of its readers. Indeed I wish the book success for both its author and its readers.

Viktor E. Frankl
VIENNA, JUNE 1967

ACKNOWLEDGMENTS

I SHOULD LIKE to thank Dr. Viktor Frankl who read each chapter as it came off the typewriter and again in its final form and who, veteran rock climber that he is, guided me over many slippery places and firmly held the rope that prevented me from sliding into the existential abyss.

I am also grateful to my wife, Judy Lieban Fabry, for correcting and typing the manuscript, and to my colleague Lucy Lawrence and to my lifelong friend and collaborator Max Knight for many editorial challenges and suggestions.

Special thanks to Mrs. Eleonore Frankl for typing, from her husband's Dictaphone, the voluminous correspondence in which he kept our dialogue open over a distance of 6,000 miles.

CONTENTS

THE PURSUIT OF MEANING

CHAPTER I

Personal Discovery

*As long as a man has a dream in his head, he cannot lose the
significance of living.* HOWARD THURMAN

AT THE AGE OF TWENTY-EIGHT, and after a sheltered middle-
class life in Vienna, I found myself in a camp for vagabonds
in Belgium. The other inmates were mostly professional people — civil servants, attorneys, businessmen, and one or two
professors. We were vagabonds only because we had entered
Belgium without a visa, after having been disenfranchised as
human beings by the Nazis in our native Austria. The year
was 1938.

We slept in dormitories, in groups of forty. Printed along
the walls, above the steel-framed cots, were quotations reflect-
ing the wisdom of the ages. "Honesty is the best policy." "Be
good and you will be rewarded." "Work by the sweat of your
brow, and you will harvest the riches." One sixty-year-old
refugee, who had been a judge for half his life, took an over-
dose of sleeping pills under a sign that said, "Do justice, and
justice will be done to you." Here, on the walls of the vaga-
bond dormitory, I came face to face with a double standard
for the meaning of life — first as it must be lived in the
presence of misery, insecurity, and apparent senselessness,
and second as it is presented by the lawmakers who write
man's moral codes: life's meaning as we experience it versus
life's meaning as man thinks it ought to be.

I had met this dilemma before. As a law student at the
University of Vienna I had come to realize that all the thousands of rules regulating our lives were based originally on
brilliantly conceived answers to human needs but that, once
codified, they offered words instead of compassion. As an attorney's apprentice it had been my job to raid the apartments

of people who were behind in their rent, and to seize any valuables I could find. Early one morning I had an experience that eventually made me give up my law career. My victim, an old man in a long nightgown, fell to his knees and begged me, the twenty-three-year-old upholder of law and order, to leave him his watch, his last family heirloom. The officer of the court, who was with me, insisted that the law left me no choice but to seize the watch.

Some other early experiences had convinced me how easily religion, too, can be taken over by the lawmakers. Early prophetic insights into man's spiritual cravings had been codified into customs and rituals. I found examples among Christian neighbors and Jewish friends. They observed the religious laws down to the finest points. A lady from a devoutly orthodox Jewish family, the owner of a hotel in an Austrian mountain resort, went to town late one Friday afternoon. On her way back, she met the mailman who, trying to save himself a climb, handed her a stack of mail for her hotel guests. When she started up the hill she noted the first star, heralding the Sabbath. Because the Talmudic laws forbid the carrying of packages on the Sabbath, she put the mail for her eighty guests on the sidewalk and went home. My young mind misinterpreted such stories as demonstrating that religion was ridiculous and meaningless. Only years later did I realize that it is the laws, customs, and rituals that make one man ridicule, look down upon, and eventually hate, another man's religion. The true meanings of a person's belief are never laughable. True beliefs unite men; desperate efforts to preserve those beliefs tear men apart.

I grew up in a city where religion had come to mean blaming the Jews for all evils, from the death of Jesus to unemployment. It always struck me as bitter irony that the Jews, who had been the first with enough imagination to replace human sacrifice with sacrificial goats, themselves had become the scapegoats.

I remember my mood of rebellion in that camp for vagabonds. Why did this happen to me? Did I deserve my suffering because of some hidden fault of which I was not aware? Or was God's justice no better than man's? Did God, too, snatch people's watches for some overdue rent owed to life? Was there no order nor justice? Was everything mere chance, whim, and chaos?

I remember my intense desire — in fact, my demand — for an answer. The response was a vast silence. While evil and injustice triumphed, some of my friends found comfort in a religion that had meant little to them in more fortunate times. One remark, made by a schoolmate I later met again in New York, sticks in my memory: "If I didn't think that there was some meaning behind it all, I'd kill myself."

I wanted to believe in meaning, in a Plan designed by a great and just Architect, but it proved difficult. My father, immediately after an operation, had been shipped to a concentration camp and had died in a cattle wagon. My mother, the gentlest person imaginable, who never knowingly had done harm to anyone, was with him and literally died of a broken heart. I rebelled. I rejected. I still was the lawyer arguing logical rebuttals. Where was sense? Justice? God was the great Lawgiver, and I had learned that laws not promulgated are not binding.

By the end of the Forties, my law career had faded into the past. I had been forced to live life, not study its case histories. Having learned a new language, I had found my way back to an earlier interest in writing and editing. And it gradually dawned on me that God was not merely a Lawgiver, but also a creative Author and Editor. Possibly He created in ways different from those of human authors who plan a story and then write according to the outline. Was it not possible that the world was designed by constant editing rather than by writing according to a plan — by hindsight rather than foresight? Man had not been created like a carefully plotted story; he had come into existence only after infinite experimentation that had also produced the tubercle bacillus, the dodo, and the giraffe. By human standards, this seems a slow and wasteful type of authorship, but for the creative force that knows no limitations of time it may have been the best. Perhaps life, too, was continuously created by constant experimentation, and perhaps man, the creature, followed this same pattern of creation — not able to see ahead, but forced to find his direction from looking backward at past experiences. Here was the possibility of a plan in the midst of apparent chaos, of meaning in the midst of meaninglessness.

The time of emigration was full of self-doubt and groping, and if a psychiatrist (or anyone else) had told me that this painful fumbling contained an element of good, I would have rejected the notion. Yet, as it turned out, the painful search turned a boy into a man. The Austrian writer Stefan Zweig, having suffered so much during his exile that he committed suicide in South America, had the perception to say, "Emigration is good for you — if you survive it." This can be said of any suffering. From suffering can come meaning.

My groping brought some comfort because it made me feel that what had happened to me was not necessarily my fault, and at the same time that I was not completely the victim of chance. Yet I felt guilty at having invented a god who was impersonal, vague, an Eternal Editor. It was a god I had created, not one who had created me. I blamed myself for being an atheist without having the courage to take the consequences of nonbelief.

Then, one Sunday morning, and quite by accident, I wandered into the Unitarian Church of Berkeley and heard my "atheism" presented by a minister, in full ministerial robes, and from a pulpit. It was not exactly my brand of atheism that was presented here as religion, but the minister expressed many of my blind gropings in straightforward words: No man can ever know the true nature of God; all concepts of God are human concepts; each person must work out the concept that confirms his own life experience; but underlying each man's beliefs must be his deep conviction that he is not alone, that he is not the victim of mere chance, that it does make a difference how he conducts himself, that he does have a place.

It was comforting, following this experience, to spend many evenings with people who were engaged in a busy search for a personal belief. God was seen in many ways: as perfection, ultimate concern, the heart of the universe, an evolving force, a father, a co-creator with man. When I mentioned my Great Editor, no one laughed and some went on to discuss the idea. I did not know it then, but this was group therapy, a great healing process.

The healing did not come about through finding new answers but through asking new questions. The question "Why did it happen to me?" remained unanswerable, and to insist on an answer led only to anguish and, worse, to fatalism. It led to the belief that because injustice and chance exist, all efforts are hopeless and there is no point in even trying. But when the question was phrased differently, the same situation that had been senseless became a challenge: "Granted that there are chance and injustice in the world, what can I — and sometimes only I — do in the situation in which I find myself?"

Again there were doubts. Was I not merely rationalizing? Fooling myself into seeing relevance and challenges where there was nothing but emptiness? Then, and again by accident, I read Viktor Frankl's book, *Man's Search for Meaning,* and later met the author in San Francisco. Once more I had the satisfaction of having my personal gropings justified by a "professional" — a psychiatrist this time, and a professor of my own Alma Mater, the University of Vienna. In the books and pamphlets he sent me I found a scholarly *Weltanschauung* that made the individual responsible for finding his own life's meaning, and called such personal discoveries a prerequisite to mental health.

I accompanied Frankl on his lecture tours in California, visited him in Vienna, and for the past four years have followed people's reactions to his message. I have been moved to see how many persons feel as lonely, bewildered, frustrated, and empty as I had felt, after my expulsion, and how desperately they are seeking a way out of the meaninglessness of their own lives. If Hitlerism was a breakdown of values and traditions, the same breakdown has now occurred in many places and under many names, even under the name of progress. And once a person experiences expulsion from whatever paradise, from whatever security, he is left to grope for meaning and order.

Logotherapy, Frankl's method of curing mental sickness, also contains a philosophy that can help people retain their sanity. William S. Sahakian, professor of philosophy at Suffolk University, said recently: "Frankl has put man in his proper place in the scheme of things, by making a human being out of him instead of reducing him, as reductionism does, to the animal level. He has restored cosmos in our thinking in place of chaos, order out of disorder, meaning out of non-sense. Finally, he is restoring sanity, in the sense that he has implanted meaningfulness in place of meaninglessness, optimism in place of pessimism and cynicism, rationality in place of irrationality."[1] In the present book I have attempted to relate this philosophy to the Western world and, especially, to the American scene. Frankl, after reading the manuscript, commented, "I find it interesting to see how you reformulate the same thoughts which I have used in my books, lively and anecdotal, and with critical explanations which apply to everyday living. Your and my formulations complement each other in such a fashion that the American reader of both your and my works will get something like a stereoscopic picture of logotherapy."

The Pursuit of Meaning may be read intellectually or existentially. It may be read for the information it contains about the philosophy underlying logotherapy, but also for its impact on the individual reader contemplating his own experiences. The reader may ask himself: "What can I learn from it in the way of general knowledge?" Or he may ask himself: "What does it mean to me personally? How does it relate to my work, to my experiences with other people, to the sufferings I have gone through, to the decisions I make, to my search for values and meanings, to the way I pursue happiness, to what I expect of life, and to how I take disappointment?"

This book presents Frankl's views on meaning and man's relationship to meaning in a world where the old guidelines of general values and traditions are fading and each individual is forced to search for his own. Accordingly, each reader will make his own personal discoveries in the ideas here offered.

What I gained from logotherapy is the recognition that central to man's life is the pursuit of meaning, and not the pursuit of happiness; that we only invite frustration if we expect life to be primarily pleasurable; that life imposes obligations, and that pleasure and happiness come from responding to the tasks of life.

I also realized through logotherapy that when the going is tough and nothing makes sense, throwing out religion solves no problem and will only hurt; in times of despair, each person will have to search for a religion that makes sense to him in his particular situation. It may be the religion of his childhood or some other established creed, but his search may also lead him outside of existing religions.

I further gained from logotherapy an awareness that this search is personal (although it can be carried on in groups or within the framework of organizations) and that each man has to engage in it even though he never can be certain that he is on the right track, or what exactly is his goal. We undertake this search in the face of ultimate uncertainty.

Finally, I achieved through logotherapy the belief that we must take life one step at a time; that we must not look for the grandiose plan, but for the challenges of the moment. With luck we shall get an occasional glimpse of the grandiose plan. The important thing is to assume that it exists.

The Beginnings of Logotherapy

Viktor Frankl was born in Vienna, in 1905. From his childhood he sensed a depth to life that went beyond material comfort. His earliest recollection is that of waking up one morning with a strong feeling of peace and security; when he opened his eyes and looked around he saw his father standing over him calmly watching him. He also remembers, as a child, sitting up one night struck by the idea that he, like everyone else, some day would die. During his school years he baffled his teachers by bringing up questions far beyond the scope of his years. In a science class, when he was fourteen, his teacher explained that life in the last analysis was nothing but a process of combustion. The boy startled the class by jumping to his feet, shouting, "If that is so, then what meaning does life have?" When another student from his high school was found dead, a suicide, with a book of Friedrich Nietzsche's nihilistic writings in his hand, Frankl realized the close connection between philosophical concepts and actual life. It confirmed his opposition to nihilism, the belief in nonmeaning which, he became convinced, was the root of despair and cruelty. The atrocities of the death camps, he maintains, were not invented in Nazi offices but in the writings of nihilistic philosophers.

Before he finished high school, Frankl had begun a scientific correspondence with Sigmund Freud which lasted for years and which led to the publication of one of Frankl's papers in Freud's *International Journal of Psychoanalysis*. As a medical student, Frankl became a member of the inner circle of Alfred Adler, the founder of individual psychology, but gradually moved away from the orthodox Adlerian view which led to Frankl's eventual exclusion from the Adlerian Society in Vienna.

The young student became increasingly dissatisfied with the narrowness of the psychiatric orientation around him. While crediting Freud with finding new insights into man and his diseases, Frankl felt that — within the circle of Viennese psychoanalysis — Freud's ideas, like so many great ideas, had begun to harden into rigid concepts. What was needed was to understand man in his totality, and Frankl set out on a career in psychiatry in which he introduced the concepts of meanings and values into psychiatric thought. "At that point," he recalled later, "I suspended what I had learned from my great teachers and began listening to what my patients were telling me — trying to learn from them."

He found many opportunities to listen to patients. After receiving his M.D. degree in 1930 he worked at the neuro-psychiatric clinic of the University of Vienna where Freud and the only Nobel Prize winner in psychiatry, Julius von Wagner-Jauregg, gave their lectures, and where Manfred Sakel developed his insulin shock therapy. In addition to his work at the University, Frankl founded youth advisory centers for distressed young people. Here the fundamental formulations of logotherapy took shape: that all reality has meaning (*logos*) and that life never ceases to have meaning for anyone; that meaning is very specific and changes from person to person and, for each person, from moment to moment; that each person is unique and each life contains a series of unique assignments which have to be discovered and responded to; that it is the search for one's specific assignments, and the response to them, that provide meaning; and that happiness, contentment, peace of mind are mere side products in that search.

Many patients in the youth centers were in despair because they could not find jobs in those years of depression. Frankl discovered that giving them a task to fulfill, such as organizing and participating in youth meetings, would relieve their despair even though these were unpaid jobs. Despair, Frankl decided, was suffering behind which the sufferer saw no meaning. But meaning can be found in a much wider range than the sufferer realizes, and it is the task of the therapist to widen the patient's horizon, to expose him to the full range of meaning possibilities. Most of those contemplating suicide who came to the youth centers saw the meaning of their lives in one direction only — the unemployed in getting work, the unmarried woman in finding a husband, the barren wife in having children. And then there were those who saw no meaning anywhere; who simply felt empty and could not bear an empty life. To explore this phenomenon of inner emptiness — the "existential vacuum," as he termed it — became the meaning of Frankl's life during the depression years in a politically unstable republican Austria which clung to the dreams of old monarchic glory. He helped his patients find perspective, rise above their narrow, selfish interests, and find meaning in their activities, paid or unpaid, and in their relationships with others. Above all, meaning could be found in accepting the unavoidable and, by doing so, turning it into a challenge. History is full of examples supporting this view: A stutterer may resign or become a Demosthenes; a blind deaf-mute may despair or become a Helen Keller; a polio cripple may withdraw from life or become President of the United States.

Trial by Holocaust

Frankl's paradise, too, ended in expulsion, but the cherubim with the fiery sword wore brown shirts with swastika armbands. The chosen people, once more, were singled out for pogrom, torture, murder, or exile. The causes of death at the hands of the Nazis were many: a whim of an SS guard; a ray of light under the door, betraying one's presence; being present at the wrong time at the wrong place when hostages were being rounded up. One had no control over these events. But added to all these uncontrollable causes of death was one more — hopelessness. To be sure, the Nazis were responsible for the hopeless situation, too, but at least one small measure of control was allowed the victim. He could not change his circumstances, but he could change his attitude toward them. Frankl introduced one of his later and still untranslated books, *Homo Patiens,* with a quote from Friedrich Nietzsche: "Not the suffering itself was his problem but that the answer was wanting to the outcry, 'Why the suffering?'" In the death camp, too, the question of "Why did this happen to me?" was bound to end in frustrated despair because no answer existed, at least not on the human level. But if the victim was able to see the holocaust as something he was forced to endure, however undeservedly, if he was able to say to himself, "All right — it happened; what can I do now?" there was at least some measure of hope. He would then see a task — to survive for the sake of a wife, to protect a child, to finish a book, to flee and defeat Nazism, or merely to survive. Survival itself became a task if behind it, perhaps unconsciously, stood the belief that some kind of order prevailed and that one could reach for it even while braving the chaos.

Such was Frankl's message, which he later expressed in his writings and which helped him survive. It is a valid message for man in any situation. If man thinks of himself as a helpless piece of debris tossed about in a wild ocean, he is likely to give up and drown. But if he thinks of himself as a human being, although shipwrecked, he will know that even in the most hopeless situation he has choices, however minute, that can make a difference. He will try to reach out for solid ground, knowing that chance and undeserved events as well as suffering, guilt, and death — the tragic triad, as Frankl calls it — are also part of life.

Frankl's expulsion took the grim form of two and a half years in German concentration camps, described in *From Death-Camp to Existentialism*, now the paperback, *Man's Search for Meaning*. His experiences in these camps confirmed the theories he had formed before, and had put into a manuscript that was to introduce logotherapy to the world. When the Nazis took this manuscript from him, he faced the prospect that neither he nor his work would survive. He escaped despair to which so many of his fellow inmates succumbed by asking himself: does the meaning of my life really depend on whether this manuscript gets published? He turned to other possible meanings, most of them immediate. The first was to survive, if possible, for the sake of his parents, wife, brother, and sister; more immediately still, his purpose was to help his fellow inmates in their despair. Although he was required to do hard labor up to eighteen hours a day, and was at one point reduced in weight to eighty pounds, he continued to practice his profession, organized secret discussion groups on mental hygiene, prompted other inmates to think about past achievements as well as tasks still waiting to be fulfilled. Hofrat Heinrich Klang, the author of the Austrian criminal law code, recalled after his liberation from the death-camp how Frankl had gathered around him a group of inmates who were, as he was himself, enthusiastic rock climbers. They had met every two weeks, and at every meeting one of them had to talk about some of his rock-climbing exploits in the Alps. Engrossed in listening, in their own memories, and their hope of seeing their mountains again, they were, for moments at least, able to rise above their hopeless situation.

Frankl's confinement in the concentration camps convinced him more than ever that each person was a unique individual who could retain a last reserve of freedom to take a stand, at least inwardly, even under the most restrictive circumstances. This seemed a painful and drastic experiment to disprove Freud's statement that when one takes different individuals and starves them, their differences are blotted out. Yet in the camps, some inmates degenerated into animals fighting for survival, while a few attained virtual saintliness by helping their fellow victims. This confirmed Frankl's belief in a dimension within each man in which he not only *is* but still decides what he will *become* in the next moment. The lesson Frankl learned in Auschwitz, and now is teaching on his lecture tours, he summarizes as follows: Even when everything that he "has" is stripped from man — family, friends, influence, status, possessions — no one can take from him the freedom to make this decision, simply because this freedom is not something that he "has" but something he "is." To this dimension of freedom man must turn in his existential despair, and to this the logotherapist must direct the patient's attention.

During a siege of typhoid fever, surrounded by dying inmates, Frankl used the mental stimulus induced by his own fever to make stenographic notes on scraps of paper, every night, to reconstruct the outline of the lost manuscript. He was able to hide the papers, and the book was later published as *The Doctor and the Soul*.

Frankl returned to Vienna, a city of despair after the wartime destruction, and swarming with Austrian Nazis. To stay there and help, he decided, was his special assignment. It was not easy to make this decision in the face of what had happened to him and his immediate family (except for one sister, all members had been killed), but he stuck to his belief that each individual must be judged on his own merits; that to condemn a group wholesale as if it were a factory lot of defective shoes is to dehumanize people, to treat them as things, whether they be Jews or Nazis. He was convinced that each person had the power and the freedom to rise above his former self, and become different, better. But even he was amazed at a dramatic example that came to his attention after the war. A physician who, under Hitler, had been responsible for the death of patients in Vienna's mental hospital, had been shipped by the Russians to Siberia. Frankl heard later that the doctor had died in a Siberian camp, beloved by his fellow inmates whom he had unselfishly served and who had never known about his past.

For Frankl, the postwar years were most creative. Within several years he published fourteen books and, in his spare time, went back to the University of Vienna to receive his second doctor's degree, in philosophy. He was given honors and recognition. He founded and became president of the Austrian Medical Society of Psychotherapy and was awarded the Austrian State Prize for Public Education. Today, at the University of Vienna, he lectures to Austrian and foreign students, a substantial contingent coming from the United States. As the head of the Department of Neurology at the Poliklinik Hospital, he supervises the work of his staff in their treatment of all in- and out-patients. He has been on lecture tours all over the world, including nineteen to the United States. He attracts audiences that fill lecture halls, school gymnasiums, and large churches. After every lecture, questions are handed to him. For days, and long after Frankl has left the lecture area, people write to and phone the sponsoring group: Where can I find a therapist in this area who practices logotherapy? Where can I read more about his methods, his philosophy, his teachings?

The answers to such questions must be disappointing. There are very few logotherapists in the United States, and there is no full-length book that explains Frankl's philosophy in layman's language — not even in German. Most of his books and all of his papers are written for the professional, and he is one of those academicians, fairly common in Europe, who believe science simplified is science falsified. In a seminar of American students he once burst out, "I can no longer oversimplify my own teachings. *Ad nauseam,* I have oversimplified them. All my talk about 'will to meaning' as against 'will to pleasure' is oversimplification in order to be understood, so that people will get an inkling of my ideas. For the sake of building bridges of understanding, I do not mind that my students continue oversimplifying my ideas; but I can't continue any longer."

This book is an attempt to build bridges — not to oversimplify, but to simplify. It is based on untranslated books, unpublished and published material, tapes of speeches, transcripts of seminars, and personal interviews. Dr. Frankl offered many factual and editorial suggestions but, as he indicated in his preface, left me free to use them or not. I therefore accept full responsibility for the contents of this book.

The Pursuit of Meaning is not written as a handbook for therapists nor as a do-it-yourself book for patients. It is written for the millions of people who are healthy but believe they are sick, because they feel empty; for those who are looking for meaning in frantic activity, in money, power, speed, excitement, sex, alcohol, and drugs, or in the pursuit of happiness for happiness' sake; for those who are looking for meaning in laws and rules and dogmas rather than searching for it personally. Every mature person has been expelled from his own paradise and lived through his own concentration camp. To help man endure this has always been the task of the prophets and priests and philosophers and educators. Now they are joined by the psychologists. Logotherapy supplies one contemporary answer to man's age-old problem of how to live after the expulsion and how to find meaning during and after the trials of suffering.

CHAPTER II

The Human Dimension

Man is an animal that makes promises to himself.
                                              FRIEDRICH NIETZSCHE

THE DICTIONARY TRANSLATION of the Greek word *logos* is "the controlling principle of the universe" or, in theological terms, "the will of God." Frankl translates it with "meaning." Logotherapy, therefore, is therapy by meaning.

As all therapies, logotherapy is based on certain assumptions about the nature of man and his place in the universe. These assumptions are being tested by Frankl and others: psychiatrists, psychologists, ministers, counselors. The medical results of logotherapy have been reported in scientific works, some of which are listed in the bibliography in the back of this book. The general appeal of logotherapy can be measured by the fact that *Man's Search for Meaning,* after an inconspicuous appearance on the American market in 1959, has now sold more than 350,000 copies. Frankl has found its effects in the most unlikely places: Trappist monks in the South of the United States use passages from it in their daily readings; a physician from South Africa, who had gone to the United States to become an obstetrician, read the book and decided to become a psychiatrist instead; and in Vienna it gave the strength to survive the ordeal of undeserved prison to a man who had been falsely accused of murder. One of the most eloquent testimonies comes from Norman Vincent Peale who predicted that "logotherapy will be recognized as the greatest advance made in a century in the old art of treating and curing human souls."[1] More cautiously, the reviewer in the *Times Literary Supplement* speculated that Frankl may belong "to a small group of human beings who are themselves so convinced of the meaning and value of existence that they can inspire others with their belief without being able to tell how and why."[2]

The Basic Assumptions

Logotherapy assumes that man, in addition to his physical and psychological dimensions, possesses a specifically human dimension, and that all three must be considered if he is to be fully understood. It assumes that this human dimension enables man to reach out beyond himself and make his aspirations and ideals part of his reality; that his life has meaning under all, even the most miserable circumstances; and that he has a deeply rooted conscience that can help him find the specific meanings of his life. Logotherapy further assumes that man primarily seeks not pleasure but life tasks, and that the deepest pleasure comes from accomplishing these tasks. It asserts that each person is unique in the sense that he has to lead his own life, that he is irreplaceable, and that no moment of his life is repeatable. Logotherapy further asserts that man is free, within obvious limitations, to make choices regarding his activities, experiences, and attitudes, and that his freedom allows him to change himself — to decide not only what kind of a person he is but also what kind of a person he is going to become. Logotherapy insists that man must not use his freedom arbitrarily, but tempered by responsibleness; that he must assume the awful and magnificent responsibility of his own choices. Finally, logotherapy contends that man's discovery of the meanings of his life is made easier by certain values and traditions passed on from generation to generation; but it asserts that the final decision is always with the individual, and that in the present era of changing values and crumbling traditions, each person is forced more than ever to rely on his personal conscience and his responsibility to listen and to follow its voice.

The first of these basic assumptions — that man has a specifically human dimension shared by no other creature — was expressed in the Bible by the image of man being created by the breath of God and as being only "a little lower than the angels." This view was generally accepted until the recent onslaught of scientific thinking which has tended to reduce man to an automaton, a puppet whose strings are pulled by biological forces and psychological drives over which he has no control. In *Homo Patiens,* one of his books not yet translated into English, Frankl wrote, "If we consider man merely as a machine ruled by conditioned reflexes, then anthropology is degraded to an annex of zoology, and the ontology of man becomes the doctrine of certain animals whose ability to walk on their hind legs has gone to their heads."

Man *can* be described in these terms but, as the German ethologist Konrad Lorenz pointed out in his book *On Aggression,* it is the instincts that are inbred into animals and men like computer programs: a salmon is "programmed" by nature to return to its place of birth to lay eggs, and we can "program" a dog to drool when we ring a bell associated with food. A man, Frankl maintains, can also be programmed, but he alone has the freedom to resist such programming. And this freedom springs from neither his body nor his psyche but from his third dimension which Frankl has called the *noëtic.*

This term has caused confusion, just as Freud's terms at first bewildered the public — the id, sublimation, the Oedipus complex. To say that the word noëtic comes from the Greek *noös* (mind, an exclusively human quality) does not explain its essence. To say that the noëtic dimension refers to the spiritual side of man, only adds to the confusion because spirit, in the English language, means not only that element in man which he does not share with other creatures, but also a manifestation of the divine. Frankl, however, uses the term noëtic only for that dimension in man which is exclusively human, and the religious connotation is misleading because the noëtic dimension exists in every man, including the non-religious. Its meaning is best explained in a simile Frankl used in a compendium of logotherapy, also still untranslated. "An airplane," he wrote, "does not cease to be an airplane when it taxis on the ground. But its true nature as an airplane becomes apparent only when it is airborne." Similarly, a man is a human being even when he moves on the merely psycho-physical plane; but he shows his essential humanness only when he rises into the noëtic dimension. This is the dimension of the uniquely human phenomena, such as love (and not mere sex); conscience (and not mere superego); meanings found and fulfilled (and not propelling drives or biological needs that must be satisfied). Animals, too, have bodies, drives, and needs, but only man has noös — more than that: he *is* noös. Noös is not acquired, nor is it a product or consequence of something else — it is man's innermost core, his self, what Christians have called "soul" and Hindus "atman" and existentialists the I in an I-Thou relationship. It is what distinguishes one person from all others. A person's noös, one might say, is his spiritual fingerprint.

But it is important to keep in mind that logotherapy does not see man as "composed" of body, mind, and spirit in terms of parts. Man is seen as a unity, and to emphasize this oneness Frankl introduced the concept of dimensions. Man is trapped in the dimension of his body, driven in the dimension of his psyche, but in the dimension of his noös he is free. Here he not merely exists, but actually influences his existence; here he is not driven but is the driver; in his noëtic dimension man decides what kind of a person he is and, more important, what kind of person he is going to become. In his noëtic dimension, man makes his choices. Only the neurotic, Frankl tells his students, misunderstands his existence as a "this-is-the-way-I-have-to-be." The healthy person has the attitude of "I-can-always-change."

Three-dimensional Man

If we disregard the noëtic dimension we get a picture not of a full man but of a caricature, an automaton of reflexes, a helpless victim of his reactions and instincts, a product of his drives, heredity, and environment. We get a *projection* of a man instead of a three-dimensional man. Frankl uses a simile with geometric bodies. From looking at a circle in a two-dimensional plane we cannot tell whether it is a projection of a sphere, of a cylinder, or of a cone. To know the true character of the geometrical body, we must consider all three dimensions. Similarly, to know a person in his fullness, we must regard him in all three dimensions: the physical, psychological, and the noëtic. If we look at a person, for instance, in his psychological dimension only, we may see a schizophrenic, having hallucinations and hearing voices. "At the same time," Frankl said in a recent lecture at Columbia University, "in a higher dimension, the same person may have accomplished a great historical achievement. Just think of Joan of Arc. For the historian, she was a person of historical achievement. For the theologian, she is a saint; she had a religious experience and encounter. . . . In the framework of psychiatry she was a schizophrenic." In a previous work he had pointed out that if the noëtic is projected into a merely psychological dimension, "the visions of a Bernadette cannot be distinguished from the hallucinations of a hysteric, and Mohammed and Dostoevski are on the same level with any other epileptic."

The danger of such reductionism has never been so great as today. The biological sciences have discovered that, indeed, we are "programmed" by our genetic setup, and determined by our glandular functions, chemical reactions, and electrical charges. The social sciences are telling us that man is the product of social and economic forces which move him about like pawns in a chess game. And psychology informs us about the drives and instincts which push us around whether we want it or not, and about the various conditioning processes which determine our behavior. Frankl does not agree with Freud's statement that man does not live but "is lived" by his instincts. Such fatalism, based on scientific thinking, is responsible for some of the dead ends in which we find ourselves. As an existential philosopher, Frankl explores existence from the point of view of personal experience. In exploring man, he starts out — as do all existential philosophers — with Descartes' *sum*, the "I am." To Frankl, the *sum* is not a biologically determined being as he was to Darwin; nor a

sociologically determined being as he was to Marx; nor a
psychologically determined being as he was to Freud. To
Frankl, man is a being who, while determined in all these
ways, retains an important area of freedom where he is not
determined at all but is free to take a stand. In his book
Logos und Existenz, he gives some contemporary examples of
where this determinism can lead. Racism, for instance, uses
biology to tell people that they are predetermined. Hitler
told the German people that man was determined by his
biology, by his "blood," and that nothing could be done about
it. If you were a Jew you were judged not on the grounds of
your social or intellectual contributions, but merely on the
grounds of biology. In Marxism it is only the sociological environment that counts. You are judged on the basis of being
either a capitalist or a proletarian. And in the United States
the tendency has developed to regard man as the outcome of
his unconscious dynamics. The views of Freud are in danger
of becoming dogma in the United States, as Hitler's were
dogma in Germany, and Marx's views are dogma in the Communist countries. The racist is certain that only our biology
determines us; the Marxist is just as certain that man's behavior is determined by his class and environment; and the
popularization and misunderstanding of Freud's ideas have
convinced many Americans that man is determined by drives
and instincts and that, correspondingly, he can be manipulated by "hidden persuaders." This has led to a fatalism in
patients that is difficult to overcome. A young girl, for instance, defended to Frankl her tendency to give up too easily,
her readiness to throw away her life, with these words, "What
can I do, Doctor? I'm just a typical only child, according to
Alfred Adler." To her this meant that no one could help her,
and least of all could she help herself, because she was stuck
with unchangeable characteristics.

Frankl does not deny that biological, social, and psychological forces have a great influence on man, but, as he once
phrased it in a filmed interview with Huston Smith, professor
of philosophy at MIT, "Man is determined, but never pan-

determined." Frankl has maintained throughout all his writings that man, even under the most restrictive circumstances, has an area in which he can determine his actions, his experiences, or at least his attitudes; and that this freedom of self-determination rests in his noëtic realm.

The Freedom to Change

This freedom gives man the opportunity to change, to step away from himself, even to confront himself. His "true" noëtic self "concerned with other beings to love and with meanings to fulfill" can face his physical and psychological organism in a confrontation that can bring about changes in attitudes. Logotherapy asserts "the defiant power of the human spirit" that enables man to resist the forces of environment and instinct, and allows him to rise above any condition that fate may bestow on him.

That this phrase is more than a mere intellectual exercise in rhetoric became evident in a talk Frankl gave to prisoners at San Quentin in California. The turnout was disappointing. Only about fifty of the more than 3,000 prisoners had assembled in the chapel, and they were not at all a captive audience. Some left during Frankl's introduction. Others seemed withdrawn and hostile. They perked up when he told about his death-camp experiences. They became attentive when he talked about the despair of prison life. These were the toughest criminals in California, many of them repeaters, but their faces stirred with emotion when Frankl told them that it was never too late, not to their last breath, to change their attitudes not only toward their fate but also toward themselves — they were not "born losers" hopelessly entangled in evil. "It lies in your power," he told them, "to step away from your former, guilty self, regardless of what happened to you in your life." A huge Negro later remarked, "He never mentioned God. He said I have it in myself to change, and maybe he is right. He's gone through it, he ought to know." Another prisoner said, "They always treat us as hopeless criminals or as psychopaths, here in prison and also outside, and so we eventually give up trying — what's the use?" A third said, "The psychologists always ask us about our childhood and the bad things in the past. Always the past — it's like a millstone around our necks. But he (Frankl) talked about what we still can do, even in prison." And then he added, "Most of us don't even come any more to hear psychologists speak. I only came because I read that he'd been a prisoner, too."

This episode does not prove that Frankl's concepts are true but merely that his approach to truth speaks to the man of today, even if he has been economically deprived, psychologically twisted, and socially rebuffed. Or perhaps just because of these handicaps. The prisoners in San Quentin were encouraged by the thought, novel to many of them, that in spite of their obvious handicaps it was still in their power to influence their fate, even if ever so slightly, to make a fresh start, to disassociate themselves from many aspects in themselves that they did not like but which they had come to consider as "millstones around their necks." And the appeal was all the stronger because such a "miracle of conversion" was possible outside the channels of religion which some of the prisoners considered meaningless at best and tools of the hated establishment at worst. A spiritual uplifting, or one might call it "noëtic uplifting," took place independent of traditional religion.

The effects of the visit were also indicated in a letter Frankl received from an inmate, the editor of the prison newspaper, *San Quentin News*. The man had written up Frankl's visit, and the article later received first place in a national penal press journalism contest. The letter said in part: "There was some local criticism of my article that went something like, 'It's fine in theory but life doesn't work that way.' I plan to write an editorial, drawing from our current situation, our immediate predicament, showing that life does indeed work this way and I shall show them an exact circumstance from prison where, from the depths of despair and futility a man was able to mold for himself a meaningful and significant life experience. They, also, would not believe that a man under these circumstances could possibly undergo a transmutation which would turn despair into triumph. I shall attempt to show them that not only is this a possibility, it is a necessity."

Noös Cannot Become Sick

The concept of the noëtic dimension helps man to understand and improve himself, and particularly helps the therapist to understand and improve mental health. The therapist must try to reach this human dimension in the patient because it contains the core of his humanity and, according to logotherapy, is the only part in the patient that never can become sick. Man's body and psyche may become sick, but not his noös. This is what Frankl calls his first, his psychiatric credo: the belief that the noëtic person exists even behind the curtain of the symptoms of a psychotic illness. If this were not so, he points out, it would not be worth the physician's while to "repair" the psychophysical organism. If he sees only the patient's organism and not also the noëtic person behind it, the physician becomes a mere medical mechanic and tacitly admits that he considers the patient as nothing but a human machine. The late psychoanalyst Franz Alexander warned physicians against developing a "plumber mentality" which repairs man like a faulty faucet.

In logotherapy, the physician elicits help from the patient's noëtic center, even if it is surrounded by his psychophysical symptoms. He evokes the defiant power of the human spirit to rebel against seemingly all-powerful forces of the psyche and the body. This is Frankl's second, his psychotherapeutic credo: the belief that not only the noëtic part of the person remains well even if the surrounding psychophysical area of the patient has become sick; but also that he, his noëtic self, has the power to rise above the afflictions of the psychophysical. He may not be able to change the condition but, again, what he *can* change is his attitude toward his own, perhaps incurably sick, psychophysical area.

On an American tour Frankl briefly met a woman who, because of incurable glandular trouble, weighed more than 300

pounds. She was ashamed to go among people, could not hold
a job, her marriage had broken up. Psychiatric treatment had
not helped. Frankl had no time for therapy but he spent an
hour talking to her. To her amazement he paid little attention
to her affliction (once he realized the incurable situation) but
stressed two points: that her condition was beyond her control
and that she would do best to take it as unchangeable; and that
she should rather give attention to all the things she still could
do, even as an overweight woman. Although he never mentioned words like "noëtic," he succeeded in making her see
that behind all that fat and those depressions triggered by her
physical condition there was her true self which still could live
a full life, in spite of her bodily handicap. "One does not have
to stand for every nonsense from oneself," Frankl told her, and
pointed out to her that she had already made a good beginning: Other people, in her place, might have become alcoholics or committed suicide. He encouraged her to take her
affliction as a challenge, to see the values life had to offer other
than physical slimness, and perhaps to become an inspiration
to other overweight women who, like herself, are trapped in
a physical situation beyond their control. A year later, when
Frankl passed through her city on another tour, the woman
came to thank him. "Your one talk did me more good than
years of treatment," she told him. She felt calmer, more hopeful, had "rejoined the human race." And, for the first time in
years, she had actually lost thirty pounds. Frankl later commented to the doctors of the hospital where the case had been
presented to him, that while her physical condition had remained incurable, existential relief had brought some small
help even in that area.

The Noëtic Unconscious

Frankl's inquiry into the noëtic dimension of man also extends into the realm of the unconscious, the great discovery of
Sigmund Freud and the broad field of study of Carl Jung.
Freud himself was aware that his explorations of human nature and its ills were only the beginnings. "I have always

confined myself to the ground floor and basement of the edifice," he wrote to his friend Ludwig Binswanger.[3] Frankl has explored the upper floors as well, but he has also made new discoveries in the basement, the unconscious. In the first paragraph of his first book, *The Doctor and the Soul,* Frankl states that "even a dwarf standing on the shoulders of a giant can see farther than the giant himself." By "standing upon the shoulders of giants," Frankl has seen heretofore undiscovered regions of the unconscious. Rising from Freud's shoulders, Frankl sees in the unconscious not only the psychological, but also an area of the noëtic. And from the shoulders of Carl Jung he sees in the noëtic unconscious not merely something collective and archetypal, but something personal and existential. Frankl sees the noëtic part of the unconscious as a region in which a man is not an ego driven by an id, but a self, a person relating to others as human beings to be loved and understood rather than as a thing to be used and manipulated.

In this noëtic realm of our unconscious we make our unconscious decisions, hold our unconscious beliefs. From here the artist draws his inspiration, the religious person his faith. Here dwells still another exclusively human quality, our sense of humor. And here, finally, we can listen to the intuitive voice of our conscience telling us our tasks and, by so doing, directing us to the meanings of our lives. And just as the psychoanalyst reaches into the patient's psychological realm of the unconscious for a diagnosis and possible cure of sicknesses originating in the psyche, so the logotherapist reaches into the patient's noëtic area of the unconscious to cure diseases originating in man's spirit, or noös. The therapist makes use of the uniquely human forces in the patient's noös: his conscience, his creative urge, his commitments, faith, intuition, and even his humor. All these can help the patient find out what is important to him, what direction he wants his life to take, and what kind of person he really is, or ought to become.

Freud pointed to the dividing line between man's con-

scious and his unconscious. Frankl adds a second dividing line
— that between his psyche and his noös. These theoretical concepts must, of course, not be visualized in any physical sense,
although it helps to imagine the dividing line between the
conscious and unconscious as horizontal and the line between
psyche and noös as vertical. The fundamental difference, however, is this: The borderline between the conscious and the
unconscious is fluid — psychoanalysis is based on the assumption that the conscious can be repressed into the unconscious
and that the unconscious can be made conscious in analysis.
The line between psyche and noös, on the other hand, is firm.
The important distinction is not whether something is conscious or unconscious, but rather whether it pertains to the id
or to the self — whether it is rooted in man's instincts and
drives, and propels him, or whether it emerges from his center
and allows him to make his own decision. Our scientific age
has made conscious reason our king and ruler, and the king
has had to face, in the first half of this century, the revolution
of the unconscious — its neglected and repressed drives (psychoanalysis), and now, in the second half of our century, the
revolution of the neglected human spirit (logotherapy).

Meaning — an Existential Answer

To the logotherapist, the human dimension is the key to man's
search for meaning. Emphasis on meaning is an existential
answer to the questions of life, and logotherapy is one of the
two major schools of existential psychiatry — the other being
Ludwig Binswanger's ontoanalysis, a method of treatment that
stresses a man's personal way of looking at his world and relating to it. But, unlike other existential psychiatrists, Frankl
has developed a practical therapeutic method; and, unlike
many psychologists in America, he builds his method on an
explicitly philosophical base. This combination of practice
and theory has attracted the attention of such leading existential philosophers as Martin Heidegger, Karl Jaspers, Gabriel
Marcel, and the late Martin Buber, and of psychologists in

many parts of the world. Among them, Gordon W. Allport, professor of psychology at Harvard University, stated in his preface to *Man's Search for Meaning:* "One cannot help but compare Viktor Frankl's approach to theory and therapy with the work of his predecessor, Sigmund Freud."

"I come from the city of Freud but not from his time." This is the way Frankl often introduces himself to American audiences. And time has changed man's attitudes and, with them, his neuroses. As Frankl never tires of pointing out, man's major problem no longer is the repression of his natural desire for pleasure, especially sexual pleasure, as was true for Freud's Victorian era; in the present sex-liberated, affluent, science-oriented, skeptical, and fatalistic society man suffers from the repression of another of his natural desires — to find meaning in his life. The repression of man's "will to meaning" causes him to feel that his life has no purpose, no challenge, no obligations; that it makes no difference what he does, that life is overpowering, that he has no more significance than an insect under a steamroller. He comes to feel that he is hopelessly trapped by circumstances beyond his control, that he is "stuck," that he has been defeated by life, that life is a rat race, a treadmill, and that there is a vast emptiness in him — Frankl's "existential vacuum." This vacuum exists among the rich and the poor, the young and the old, the successes and the failures. As logotherapists could show, business executives try to fill it with extra work, their wives with parties and bridge games, students with marijuana or LSD. The existential vacuum lurks behind many of man's feverish attempts to fill his emptiness — with sex, alcohol, defiance of authority, speedy cars, committee work, television watching, overeating, and even with such respected activities as politics, psychoanalysis, and religion. The feeling of emptiness is especially widespread among the youth. Forty percent of Frankl's Austrian students and 81 percent of his American students confessed to it, and similar figures have been reported in other universities. The existential vacuum was prominent in a survey of 100 prosperous Harvard alumni: one-fourth of them doubted that their lives had any meaning, and the same doubt was reported in Czech journals of psychiatry as existing also in the Communist countries.

The existential vacuum, however, is no disease. The repression of man's will to meaning does not bring on neurosis any more than a repression of his will to pleasure automatically leads to sickness. On the contrary, as we know since Freud, the repression of sexual desire can be a great human achievement if it is done for the sake of a higher value — a man's respect and love for a girl, or a priest's respect and love for God. Frankl disagrees with Freud's statement that to doubt the meaning of life is a symptom of sickness; on the contrary, such doubting may trigger a man's search for meaning, and logotherapy uses his thirst for a meaningful existence to maintain or recover mental health.

Frankl's audiences respond with relief when he assures them that a feeling of inner emptiness is by no means a symptom of mental disease but, on the contrary, a challenge to fill this emptiness — a challenge to which only a human being can rise. At the present, when so many people are becoming psychological hypochondriacs, always looking for childhood traumas, rejections, and other psychological excuses for their failures and confusions, they find strength in the message that their feeling of meaninglessness is not a symptom of sickness but proof of their humanness: Only man can feel the lack of meaning because only he is aware of meaning.

However, there is danger. Into this existential vacuum mental disease may enter. Doubting the meaning of life may lead to despair, depression, and a new type of neurosis for which Frankl has coined a new term — "noögenic" neuroses. These are neuroses that do not originate in the psyche of the patients and are not brought about by such traditional Freudian causes as repressed sexuality, childhood traumas, or conflicts between different drives or between the id, ego, and superego. Noögenic neuroses originate in man's noëtic dimension and may be brought about by value collisions, by conflicts of conscience, or by the unrewarded groping for man's highest value — an ultimate meaning of life. Psychologists at Harvard University and at Bradley Center, Columbus, Georgia, developed tests to distinguish between such noögenic neuroses and other, more conventional, forms. The Georgia tests, using 1,200 patients, consistently support Frankl's thesis that we are really dealing with a new syndrome.[4] In these cases, the orthodox approach of psychoanalysis of going back to the past to search for causes hidden in the psyche will be of little avail. Noögenic neuroses respond to a therapy that draws the patient's awareness to the present and the future, to commitments to fulfill, relationships to establish, and meanings to find — in other words, they respond to logotherapy.

A New Type of Neurosis

It is central to Frankl's beliefs that every man, as a noëtic person, can solve clashes of conscience and value conflicts by himself, and that the logotherapist's role is merely to help him solve them by convincing him that he is *not* the helpless victim of his upbringing, surroundings, and inner drives, but that he can take a stand, as the healthy person will. It is, however, possible that value conflicts or "existential frustration" can overwhelm a person and lead to neurosis, as for instance in a case described by Frankl in *Theorie und Therapie der Neurosen*. Here he had to deal with the conflict of a mother who was torn between the demands of her church to bring up her children in a certain faith, and the demands of her husband to raise them in the atheistic tradition in which he had grown up.

In our era of swift changes, an increasing number of people are being caught between "old" and "new" values: The church-supported virtue of having many children versus the call to help prevent a potentially disastrous population expansion; the virtue of virginity versus the approval of one's own "gang"; the value of making a career (even if it depends on becoming a yes-man) and the value of independence; the value of a well-paying, though meaningless, job versus the value of

following one's calling to become an artist; the value of growing roots in a community versus that of a profitable career
after a transfer out of town. It is significant that in recent years
the conflicts of people often have to do with job security,
salaries, and material goods versus such "old-fashioned" values
as taking over the family business, excellence of workmanship,
and rugged individualism. Psychiatrists have observed that
even the anxieties of so-called endogenous depressions have
changed during recent years. One generation ago, many
patients blamed themselves, feeling guilty before their conscience, their father and mother, their community, or before
God. As Frankl indicates in *Psychotherapy and Existentialism,*
today's endogenously depressed patients are worried more
about their health, their ability to earn money, to keep up
their payments. They display anxieties connected with their
jobs, their getting old. Frankl once quipped that depressive
patients nowadays are concerned less with the Day of Judgment and more with payday.

To understand, diagnose, and possibly cure noögenic neuroses, logotherapy was developed. But, equally important, the
concepts that led to the development of logotherapy help us
take a new look at man — not only at neurotic man but simply
at man, with his struggles, ambitions, failures, and triumphs
— a look at man and his lifelong pursuit of meaning.

CHAPTER III

What Is the Meaning of Life?

Only a life lived for others is worthwhile.

ALBERT EINSTEIN

FEW THINGS IRRITATE FRANKL as much as the question, "What *is* the meaning of life?" The question has haunted him all his life, and he has spent all his life trying to answer it. He tells the story of how, early in his career as a psychiatrist and youth counselor, a schoolmate called him on the phone: "Say, Viktor, I am here with a friend who wants to commit suicide because he can't see any sense in living — tell me quickly, what shall I tell him *is* the meaning of life?"

The question crops up, in various forms, after every one of Frankl's talks. He knows, of course, that this question is the crux of today's anxiety, and its answer the crux of logotherapy. But Frankl's important point is that each man can answer it only for himself, and never for more than the moment. For the man and the situation are constantly changing, and with them the meaning that he is required to fulfill.

Meaning Implies Commitment

From some of his writings, one gets the impression that Frankl uses the word "meaning" where traditional writers speak of the "will of God." In most instances, however, he uses it in the sense of commitment. It is one of logotherapy's contributions that it is widening the areas in which meanings can be found. For centuries the search for meaning was restricted to the religious area, and very often to a set of specific creeds or dogmas; the nonbeliever (of a specific approach to truth) was condemned to the hell of meaninglessness. But psychiatry, as a branch of medicine, cannot restrict its healing methods to the religious, and even less to the sectarian. As Frankl has often stressed, the therapist is obliged, if by nothing else than by his oath of Hippocrates, to help all patients alike. If the cure consists, as logotherapy maintains, in helping the patient to find meaning in his life, then the nonreligious patient has as much right to expect help as the religious. And the religious therapist has no right to lead the atheistic patient onto the religious path to find meaning; nor has the atheistic therapist the right to discourage his religious patient from finding meaning through faith. All the therapist can do is to elicit in the patient the widest range of meaning potentials, encourage him to make his choices, and educate him to make responsible choices. Logotherapy has been defined by Frankl as education to responsibility and this in an age where technology threatens to reduce man to a thing which has no responsibility, only reactions.

Logotherapy, however, puts into a contemporary language what religious leaders, philosophers, and artists have said in many ways: Man reaches out. He is a creature in pursuit of goals. He alone is aware of a higher dimension that beckons him, and he finds fulfillment in answering the call. What is he reaching for? Some wise men have found inspired answers, but the mass of people has been groping blindly. And so the priests, the oldest lawgivers, captured the precious findings of wisdom, preserved them in dogmas and rituals, and thus narrowed them into channels accessible to the masses. Perhaps this is the only way to preserve inspiration; for apparently only a few can experience eternal truths directly. Others can see only the colorful trappings of rituals and symbols. And eventually the symbols, and not the truths and wisdoms behind them, become the object of worship and belief. The worship of the colorful trappings instead of the wisdom they contain apparently is as old as written records will show. St. Paul said, "We have this treasure in earthy vessels," which Bishop James A. Pike interprets as saying, "Meanings have to be carried in some kind of package . . . but it's very important that we do not worship the vessels."[1]

Meaning as an Anchoring Place

For the most part it didn't seem to matter what people believed as long as they were sincere in their belief. What mattered was the awareness that there is more to life than the world of things; that beyond the material world lies another which has been given a variety of religious and nonreligious names, and which to Frankl is a world of meanings, values, ideals, goals, and purposes. We reach out for this unseen world, beyond animal dimension, and even beyond human dimension. Being human, and being subject to human limitations, we cannot clearly see what the goals are. We are like the boy in the Indian rope-trick act. He climbs up the rope the magician has flung into the air although no one can see the anchoring place and no one even knows for certain that such a place exists. Man climbs up on faith that the rope has found an anchoring place in unknown dimensions.

Man has believed in a great variety of anchoring places, and these beliefs have given him purpose, security, happiness, and sanity. The rope has been anchored in Zeus and the Greek gods who personally took part in man's life, or in Jahwe who made a personal pact with his people, or in Jesus who promised personal salvation to the believers. But every age outgrew its static beliefs because man and his knowledge about himself and his universe are dynamically evolving. Whenever this new knowledge outdistances man's traditional beliefs, a period of doubt, despair, and frustration sets in. Such a period of crisis is overcome when reality is faced honestly, the old traditions are scrutinized, the obsolete is eliminated, and fresh truths are discovered by the wisest men of the era — to redirect man's beliefs to anchoring places more in line with the knowledge of the day.

We live in such a period of crisis. Man's knowledge about his nature and his place in reality has been changing fundamentally and fast. He experiences a "Copernican switch" — from the belief that he is the center of the universe to the realization that he is but an insignificant part of the periphery.

It took centuries for man to digest the Copernican truth, but other blows to our egocentric concepts followed in accelerating succession — Galileo, Newton, Darwin, Freud, Einstein. The last two are, for all practical purposes, our contemporaries; and yet their discoveries have already become part of our thinking and beliefs. What we know about the world we live in has radically changed within one generation. The world in which we shall die is not the same into which we were born. Our parents' generation, born in the horse-and-buggy age, lived long enough to die in the jet age. Our own generation, born in the Model-T age, will die in the moon-rocket age, and beyond. Our children can no more imagine what life in the pre-Freudian era was like than we can imagine what it was like to live in the times before Newton. Even our method of acquiring new knowledge has undergone a basic change. Scientific man is prone to accept truths not by faith but by scrutiny. We are less likely to accept what Bishop Pike calls "prefab truth" that comes from sacred books and wise men of the past. Modern man is looking for truths that can be researched in repeatable experiments. What this does to religion, which is based on unrepeatable personal experiences, we are only beginning to understand. The impact of scientific thinking makes us disregard phenomena that cannot be measured but are subject to judgment and faith. At first glance, this seems to destroy religion, but in the long run religion will be strengthened because it is being placed on foundations that stand up not only in the dark shrines of the churches but also in the bright laboratories. Even our scientists do not insist on proving everything they discover, for the scientific method also calls for hypotheses and assumptions. And we are beginning to realize that what can be seen through the telescopes and under the microscopes strengthens rather than destroys the fundamentals of our age-long beliefs because it brings our beliefs into focus with reality as it emerges in our era. What need to be discarded are the old shells and wrappings, so that we can reexamine the valid contents. If, in our awe for science, we declare that "God is dead," we simply state that our prescientific concepts of God are as dead as the Egyptian sun god and Zeus. But, as Paul Tillich pointed out, God may be dead, but divinity is not. Divinity has always been the same, but our awareness of it has changed. For thousands of years we have kept reaching out for dimensions beyond human experiences, no matter what we call the anchoring place of the rope.

In our present age of science, the inspired searchers of old, the prophets, sages, and artists, are joined by the scientists to provide contemporary answers to ancient questions. Among the scientists offering new answers are the psychiatrists. Frankl's answers are based on the assumption that individuals, even in our era of doubt and nonfaith, still must find bases for insight, courage, and decisions to make, and that ancient valid truths must be combined with current views of the physical sciences, existential philosophy, and mental health.

Three Tenets of Logotherapy

Logotherapy is based on three tenets which perhaps cannot be proved but certainly may be experienced. Although doubted by some, they have been found acceptable by a wide range of people — from Jesuits and orthodox Jews to atheists and agnostics. The tenets are: Life has meaning under all conditions; man has the will to reach out for meaning and feels frustrated or empty if this will is not applied; and man has the freedom, within obvious limitations, to find the meaning of his life.

Logotherapy sees man as a being whose life consists of a string of situations, each of which has a specific meaning for him, and him alone. His fulfillment, happiness, and even mental well-being depend on finding, to the best of his capacities, the meaning of each situation of his life. He may find these meanings in the framework of religious orthodoxy, religious liberalism, humanism, atheism, or agnosticism — it makes no difference. What does make a difference, though, is his awareness that he is free to seek the meanings of his life, that he has the obligation to do so, and that no one can do

it for him. The pursuit of the unique meanings of his life
makes each individual a unique personality — a chosen person, as it were, not because he belongs to a certain religion
or nation, but because he is a man.

As often, Frankl draws on the Old Testament and ancient
Jewish writers to support his views. He is fond of a passage by
the Jewish teacher Hillel, a contemporary of Jesus. Hillel told
his students: "If I don't do it, who will do it? If I don't do it
now, when shall I do it? And if I do it for myself, what am I?"
These three questions present the essence of logotherapy. The
first part says, "I am irreplaceable." The second, "Each moment is unique and won't come back." And the third stresses
that if I do a job only for my own sake, I am not true to my
human nature. Frankl likes a phrase by Shlomo Bardin, executive director of the Brandeis Institute, California, who calls
men the "trustees of life." Each person is responsible to carry
out, to the best of his abilities, what is entrusted to him, to
develop his potentials, to make the best of his life, to use it
as a great opportunity — in fact, as the German poet Friedrich
Hebbel put it, "Life is not something but rather an opportunity for something." To Frankl, man's will to meaning is his
primary human motivation, and the pursuit of meaning his
inalienable right. Meaning is the anchoring place for the rope.

In a seminar, a student challenged Frankl's concept that
man's will to meaning was more basic than his will to pleasure.
The newborn baby, the student said, obviously has a will to
pleasure but no will to meaning. This, Frankl replied, was
not a valid argument. It was just like saying that crying is
more basically human than speaking because a baby, before
it can speak, shows a great capacity for crying. "Something
may be basically human and yet manifest itself only in later
stages of development," he concluded.

Pragmatic Approach

Logotherapy approaches the question of meaning from every
direction, from the scientific, the religious, the philosophical,
and the existential.

The search for meaning starts on a simple, day-by-day

level. A man can find meaning by responding to the situation of the moment, by accepting the simple tasks of his life. This point was illustrated by Frankl to an American newspaperman who interviewed him in his study at the Poliklinik Hospital in Vienna: "We are united here in the same situation. Yet the meanings are different. For me, the meaning of the situation is to make logotherapy clear to you. For you, it is to understand what I am saying so that you can pass on this information to your readers. To my nurse, the meaning of this same situation is to keep visitors away and answer the phone so we can talk undisturbed. And an hour from now the meaning of the moment might be for me to see a patient, while for you it might be to go sightseeing in Vienna, and for my nurse to make appointments for patients."

This pragmatic approach to the problem of meaning was discussed at a meeting on logotherapy held among scientists in the San Francisco Bay Area. One chemist pointed out that Frankl's way was the way of science. "He states the hypothesis that life has meaning. Then he encourages the patient to take a lamp and step into the dark. He will see only a very limited circle of light around him. Then Frankl suggests that the patient hold his lamp higher and take further steps, one at a time, as his surroundings become visible. In this manner, eventually, he may find his path."

This is the task of the logotherapist: to illuminate, to let meaning "shine forth." But behind the simple meanings of the moment lie larger tasks. In the Vienna interview, for instance, beyond the immediate task of discussing logotherapy and keeping disturbances out, there were the larger tasks: For Frankl, to spread the message of logotherapy; for the newspaperman, to write a series of articles; for the nurse, to help her doctor. And still further beyond lay even more universal tasks: to speak to the needs, and cure the ills, of our age; to be a truthful reporter; to be a conscientious nurse. One has to start with the first step: One cannot be a great physician without paying careful attention to the specific moment and to the individual patient at hand.

This attention to the present and the immediate step

ahead characterizes Frankl's philosophy and is evident in his daily conduct. He often talks about his favorite hobby, rock climbing in the Alps. On the steepest precipice he never gives a thought to how high he still has to climb or how deep he might fall. He concentrates on the immediate task ahead: to find the next firm grip, the next foothold. To worry about the distant difficulties, he says, would only result in paralyzing anxiety.

Meaningful Activities

All meanings mentioned so far lie in the realm of activities, one of the three areas in which, according to logotherapy, man can find meaning. Activities can give a man meaning in various ways — through his job, through hobbies, through deeds he does for the sake of others. The "beloved" work is meaning-fulfilling if it is done for the sake of the work itself and its effect on the worker and the people he cares for. "Beloved" work is never merely a means to an end — to make money, to gain status or power. Today fewer and fewer jobs provide their holders with meaningful activities; they do not challenge the worker as a human being but only provide him with the opportunity to function (and not very efficiently) as part of a machinery. There still is meaning-fulfilling work — that of a research scientist, a physician, a policy-making executive, a teacher, or a creative artist. Yet, the holders of routine jobs, too — a factory worker, a clerk, a salesgirl, a housewife — may be able to see relevance in their work. A patient in the Poliklinik Hospital once expressed what probably many feel when Frankl talks to them about the meaning of their work: "It's easy for you, Professor, you are a psychiatrist, you can find meaning in your work. But what can I find in mine, as a carpenter?" Frankl told him that a carpenter who fulfills his task to the limits of his capabilities can find as much meaning as a physician who fulfills his job the best he can; and that the activities of a housewife can be as meaningful as those of an artist. What matters is not the kind of work but the motivation: the artist whose main goal is to make money with work that remains below his best talent will lead a less meaningful life than the housewife who keeps house for the sake of her husband and children. "What matters," Frankl has said often, "is not how large is the radius of your activities, but only how well you fill its circle."

But even with the best intention it sometimes is difficult to find meaning in one's particular work. Fortunately, with working hours becoming shorter, people have more opportunity to find meaningful activities during their leisure hours — for instance, through adult education courses, volunteer work for hospitals, community or neighborhood improvement, precinct work for a political party, or artistic activities. However, people must watch out that these activities have the purpose of filling their existential vacuum, and not of running away from it.

But changing jobs is not always the solution: it may not solve, but create noögenic conflicts in the jobholder as well as among members of his family. Such conflicts are sometimes brought about by the policy of some companies to move their executives up the ladder by moving them around the country, and even abroad. The sales manager of an automobile company who was transferred every few years to a different area suffered a nervous breakdown whose noögenic origin was illuminated through a recurring dream in which he saw himself as a car that was turned in annually for a new model. The wife of an engineer became the victim of a depression when her husband was made supervisor and was transferred to a small company town where she had no friends, at exactly the time when her children left home to marry and go to college. The seven-year-old girl of an executive of an oil company began to stutter after her father had been promoted three times in two years, every time moving to a different city. But job conflicts are not restricted to the executive level. The simplest kind of job may cause a clash between material and human values. Often a person takes on work that was satisfying to him in his youth but, as he matures, no longer challenges him. He then must decide whether to "fill the circle" of his present activities or to make a break for a job with higher challenges. A thirty-five-year-old ex-toolmaker said, "I hate that eighteen-year-old boy who decided that I should become a toolmaker. Not that I was a failure. I was the best toolmaker possible, and if I had been married and had children, I probably would have remained a toolmaker for the sake of my family. But I felt that I could make a better contribution as a teacher, so I quit my job and went back to college." A biochemist, at the age of 42, married and a father of three, gave up the tenure of a full professorship and went back to a divinity school to become a minister (and later insisted on taking a church in a slum area). A composer gave up a $50,000-a-year job in Hollywood, and now lives in the Big Sur area with his wife and four children, writing folksongs on subjects he feels are important, such as civil rights, conservation, and peace, and refuses to make commercial use of even these compositions. "If you want to hear my songs," this twentieth-century troubadour tells people, "you have to invite me to your living room or to your church." A minister who felt that his true beliefs no longer conformed to what was expected of him by his denomination and by the elders of his church, accepted a minor position in a more liberal denomination. All these examples from contemporary California seem to illustrate Frankl's point that, while man cannot choose the meanings of his life, he can choose the commitments that will bring him meaning.

The Meaning of Personal Experience

The second area in which, according to logotherapy, man can find meaning, is the area of experiences such as beauty, truth, or love. Unlike activities, where meaning is found by active participation, experiences provide man with meaning by receiving. Frankl remembers the "spiritual shivers" he felt when, at the age of sixteen, he read Freud's *Beyond the Pleasure Principle*. This was an experience of truth discovered. He also recalls what it had meant to him to suddenly see the sunset through the barbed wire of the concentration camp — an experience of beauty. But the greatest experience is that of mature love — to know just one single human being in all his uniqueness. It matters little how long such experiences last. "One moment," Frankl maintains, "can retroactively flood an entire life with meaning." It is like a curtain opening for one second, allowing a glimpse of the rope anchored in a dimension usually beyond human vision.

In his book, *The Doctor and the Soul,* Frankl points out that love presents man with a gift that he has otherwise to get by effort: his uniqueness. Love means that someone is stepping up to one individual, selecting him from among the three billion people on earth, and saying to him, "You, and no one else." It is logotherapy in full action: according to Frankl's concept, the lover sees not only the present "Thou" of the beloved, but also the potential the beloved is free to become. "Love helps the beloved to become as the lover sees him," is the way he put it. If I may be allowed to present my own experience as a "case history": I arrived in New York, a penniless refugee, jobless at the tail end of the Depression, an ex-attorney with knowledge of laws no longer existing in even my own country, a writer without a language. I met a girl who did not care what I had (or did not have) and who perceived what I was — what I could become if only someone believed in me. She did not tell me this; she acted upon it by marrying me.

To find meaning in experiences need not always have such exalted overtones as finding truth, beauty, or love. A teen-ager can experience meaning by listening to the Beatles, Frankl suggested. "Why not? The teen-ager finds meaning because he loves the Beatles. I find it by listening to Gustav Mahler. To each his own." As a music enthusiast, he often poses the rhetorical question: If you were listening to a supreme rendering of your favorite symphony, and someone tapped your shoulder and asked you whether life has meaning — could there be any other answer than "yes"? The same answer would be given by the nature lover on a mountain top, the religious person at a memorable service, the intellectual at an inspiring lecture, the artist in front of a masterpiece, and the scientist at the moment of discovery.

The Meaning of Attitudes

That meaning can be found in activities and experiences is easily perceived. More difficult to see is Frankl's contention that meaning can also be found in a third area — man's attitudes; that, indeed, the deepest meaning can be found here. Finding meaning in attitudes becomes important when man is facing Frankl's "tragic triad" — unavoidable suffering, inerasable guilt, and death. This does not mean that anyone should go and look for meaning by looking for suffering — that would merely be meaningless masochism. But where a person is faced with a painful situation which cannot be altered, he can find meaning in facing it bravely and with dignity, setting an example to others in similar predicaments, turning the suffering into an ultimate achievement of the human spirit, for the sake of some person or some cause. The deaths of Jesus and Socrates and Leonidas have been inspirations for thousands of years, giving testimony to the meaning found in the suffering of death for the sake of love, justice, and patriotism. History is full of stories about heroes and martyrs who turned tragedy into triumph. The story is told about Tristan Bernard, the French writer, who, together with his wife, was taken to the Drancy concentration camp by the Nazis. While they were marching in a column of despairing Jews, Bernard said to his wife, "Up to now we have lived in fear; from now on we will live in hope." From the depth of a situation of despair, he had reversed the entire outlook of the situation, not by changing the situation but by changing his attitude. And his example helped his fellow sufferers to shoulder their lot with courage. Given a cause, even the ordinary man may become a hero. Examples from contemporary history show how the British stood up under the blitz during World War II, and how the Berliners braved the privations during the airlift. They were aware of a meaning behind their suffering, and of the example they set for the rest of the world.

No birth is without labor pains, figuratively and literally. The history of creative people is full of tales of pain, from Michelangelo's "agony and ecstasy" to Handel's complete physical exhaustion upon giving birth to his *Messiah*. Frankl speaks of the struggle of the genuine artist who is not satisfied until his hundredth draft of his creation or the tenth version of his work has stood the test of his artistic conscience. It is also questionable whether the moments of bliss in a love relationship could be possible without the "labor pains" of agony and doubt. Yet no true artist would forego his creation, nor the lover his love, because pain is the price. And neither would a mother forego her child because she knows that she will have to endure what is probably the most universal human "suffering" in the world. On the contrary: She is happily suffering pain for the sake of having a child. Imagine, however, her anguish were she to know in advance that her baby was going to be a lifelong Mongolian idiot. Yet, when in some unfortunate cases she is faced with the unavoidable fact that her child is an incurable idiot, many a woman will turn this suffering into an achievement by devoting her love to her child, setting an example to other parents in similar tragic circumstances. It is not the load that breaks us down, logotherapy seems to say, but the way we carry it.

Turning suffering into an achievement, setting an example, thinking of others, providing inspiration, are not pious words of advice but crucial issues in therapy. The effectiveness of Alcoholics Anonymous is based on the idea of setting examples and giving help to others. Many a grief-stricken parent has found solace from the death of a child by establishing scholarships enabling other young people to get the education his own child had missed. Stanford University is a memorial from a father who had been able to find meaning behind the incomprehensible death of his son by turning from self-centered sorrow to the joy of providing education for entire generations.

How Logotherapy Deals with Suffering

Logotherapy cannot stop unavoidable suffering but it can stop despair, which Frankl defines as suffering behind which the sufferer sees no meaning. Suffering itself has no meaning; but a person can assume meaningful attitudes toward events which themselves are meaningless.

The meanings that patients can find in unavoidable suffering must be found on the patient's, and not the doctor's terms. The nonreligious person will discover meanings in a variety of ways — for the sake of a child, a friend, his country, a scientific discovery, or to inspire others. Heroes in literature, from Oedipus to Hamlet, found meanings behind their suffering, guilt, and death. Goethe, the outstanding humanist of the eighteenth century, seemed to have anticipated logotherapy when he said, "There is no condition which cannot be ennobled either by a deed or by suffering." *Faust,* Goethe's life-work, can easily be interpreted in terms of logotherapy: Bored, frustrated, and beset by conflicts of conscience, Faust attempts to fill his existential vacuum by selling his soul to the Devil, with the understanding that the Devil will help Faust in his search for meaning. The Devil tries sex, wealth, power, but not until Faust experiences and shares the suffering of mankind, and, turning away from self-centered pleasures, finds meaning in providing living space for the sake of an overcrowded population, does he find fulfillment.

The religious person, too, can find meaning behind suffering in a variety of ways, and it is an oversimplification to say that he will find it for the sake of God. Here, too, the doctor must allow the patient to find meaning on the patient's own terms. This is illustrated in the case of an orthodox rabbi who had lost his wife and his six children in the concentration camp at Auschwitz. He had married again and was in deep despair because his second wife was sterile, thus he could not have a son to say the traditional Jewish prayers after his death. Frankl, trying to kindle hope in the patient, asked him if he did not expect to see his children in Heaven, according to the patient's religious convictions. The question resulted in an outburst of tears, and now the true reason for the despair came to the fore: his children had died as innocent martyrs for the glory of God, and thus would be found worthy of the highest place in Heaven. He, however, as an old sinful man, could not expect to be assigned to the same place. During the ensuing conversation, Frankl suggested the possibility that this might have been precisely the meaning of his survival: an opportunity to be purified from sins by the years of suffering the children's loss, so he too, although not innocent as his children, might become worthy of joining them in Heaven. Was it not written in the Psalms that God preserved all our tears? For the first time the rabbi saw the possibility of meaning behind his sufferings in his own religious terms. He left the logotherapeutic session with fresh hope that, after all, his suffering might not have been in vain.

How logotherapy can deal with the problem of unavoidable suffering is also illustrated by the quite different case of Sister Michaela of the rigid Catholic Order of the Carmelites. She suffered from severe depressions and had considered suicide. She particularly suffered from her feeling of guilt based on her belief that, as a good Christian, her faith should be strong enough to conquer her sickness. Frankl diagnosed her disease as what is called in psychiatry, "endogenous" depression. Accordingly, he prescribed those drugs modern pharmaco-psychiatry uses for such cases. When talking to the patient, however, he also stressed that her depression had a primarily organic cause; hence she was not responsible for it. Thus, the fact that she suffered from the depression was not due to any failure on her part. How she took it, however, could very well constitute an intellectual and spiritual achievement.

After a few therapeutic sessions, the patient was relaxed and in better spirits. She remarked, "I am at peace with myself and grateful. I have accepted this cross." She later showed Frankl an entry in her diary which he treasures as a testimony to the defiant power of the human spirit. It reads in part:

I am exposed to unknown forces which overwhelm my will
— quite helplessly exposed I am. Sadness is my steady companion: whatever I do, it weighs me down like lead upon my
soul. Where are my ideals? Gone — as all the good and beautiful things for which I used to strive. Nothing but yawning
boredom fills my heart. I live as if thrown into a vacuum,
and at times not even pain is accessible to me. In this distress I call God, the Father of all, and even God is silent. I
wish for only one thing — to die. If I had not the faithful
awareness that I am not the master over my life, I would
have ended it many times; but through this awareness the
bitterness of my sufferings is suddenly transmuted. For, a
person who assumes that his life must consist of stepping
from success to success is like a fool who stands next to a
building site and shakes his head because he cannot understand why people dig deep down when they set out to build
a cathedral. God builds a temple out of each man's soul, and
in my case he is just starting out to excavate the foundations.
It is my task to offer myself to His excavations.

In emphasizing the meaning potential of suffering, in the
United States Frankl runs contrary to the current tendency of
a society that is so success- and happiness-centered that people
are apt to hide their suffering as if it were something shameful.
Suffering as a possible source of achievement is likely to be
rejected by a nation that answers the question of "How are
you?" automatically with a smile and an "I'm fine," regardless. When Frankl lectured the first time to an American
scientific society, he spoke of the meaning that can be elicited
in people when they face suffering and death bravely and with
dignity, and he felt that his audience rejected his idea. After
the lecture, one of the leading Horney psychiatrists told him,
"Dr. Frankl, don't be surprised that they fight you — they
envy you because you have suffered and they have not." He
later was told the same thing when he lectured at Harvard.
But since then, some American psychiatrists have spoken up in
support of Frankl's positive attitude toward the unavoidable
fact of human suffering. Edith Weisskopf-Joelson of Duke
University has pointed out that Frankl's value system "may

help to counteract certain trends in our present-day civilization, where the incurable sufferer is given little opportunity to be proud of his unavoidable and incurable suffering, and to consider it ennobling rather than degrading."[2]

Perhaps the meaning of suffering cannot be understood by logic alone; it has to be experienced. Frankl's favorite statement comes from Yehuda Bacon who as a boy survived the Auschwitz death camp and now is an artist in Israel. When he was liberated from the camp, it had been his ambition to tell everyone what had happened, so it would not happen again, and thus make the world a better place. But he soon found out that people did not want to know. He realized that, as far as improving mankind was concerned, his suffering had been in vain. But he found meaning in another area. "Suffering can have a meaning," he wrote, "if it changes *you* (the sufferer) for the better."

Ultimate Meaning

Frankl maintains that man's attitudes, even more than his activities and experiences, provide him with the opportunity to find life's deepest meaning. Although it is possible to find meaning through creative activity and personal experiences, it is by our attitudes, when facing unavoidable suffering, that we express our belief in "ultimate meaning," existing on the highest possible level. Perhaps only such a belief, even when it remains unconscious, enables us to turn suffering into an achievement. It is no great achievement to work successfully and love happily, but to see meaning in the face of suffering is an achievement; however, such an achievement seems to be possible only if we have a trust that ultimate meaning exists in spite of all evidence to the contrary on the human level. In unavoidable suffering we are stripped down to the essentials, we no longer are concerned with the impressions we make on others, with compromises, or long-range designs. The experience of tragedy calls us to the root of our life and can become a turning point from the superficial to the profound. Only when we face tragedy will we show whether the meanings we have embraced are conditional or ultimate.

The concept of ultimate meaning has brought to Frankl the accusation of "sneaking in religion by the back door." If we understand by religion a belief in ultimate meaning located in a dimension beyond man, then the accusation has substance. But the belief that there is more to reality than man and his human dimension has been asserted not only by the religious leaders but also by atheistic philosophers and existential theologians. The belief that there is something greater than man has been expressed in many ways, from Nietzsche's "Man must overcome himself and strive toward Superman," to Tillich's and Barth's insistence that man is not the ground of his being. Frankl's belief in meaning is existential, based on experience, though backed by observations in hospitals and concentration camps. These observations have strengthened his belief in man's inborn faith in meaning — that, as he puts it, man could not even breathe or move a limb without being permeated, down to his biological roots, by a belief in meaning, or what Frankl calls a basic trust in ultimate meaning.

He also found (and his findings were supported by Walter Ritter von Baeyer, the head of the Psychiatric Department of the University of Heidelberg) that agnostics, on their deathbeds, exhibited a strange tranquility and security, which could not be explained in terms of their agnostic views, but only by a trust in ultimate meaning — a trust which exceeded rationalization within the framework of their agnosticism. Ultimate meaning is an axiom which cannot be proved but must be assumed; a belief in an ordered world despite the obvious fact that life on the human level is confusing, irrational, unsystematic, contradictory, and full of whims and chances. A similar conviction was expressed by Albert Einstein when he said he could not believe that God played dice with the universe.

Meaning Is Found, Not Fabricated

If the deepest, the ultimate, meaning is understood in this manner, Frankl's repeated emphasis that meanings must be found rather than invented, becomes a logical next step. Others can give us example and inspiration, but not meaning. Meaning cannot be given by a parent, teacher, or friend; it cannot be dictated by a leader, nor can it be prescribed by a minister or therapist. And no one can give it to himself. No one can suddenly declare: "Enough of this meaningless life! From now on I'll have meaning." In Frankl's view, we cannot "will" meaning in this general manner any more than we can will faith or love. As with these, meaning also must come in response to something or someone outside us. It must come in response to what the gestalt psychologist Max Wertheimer has called the "requiredness of the situation."[3] All we can do is to be open to meanings, to make a conscious effort to try to see all the possible meanings that a situation offers us, and then select the one which, to the best of our limited knowledge, we consider the true meaning of that particular situation.

Here Frankl runs into a dilemma. On the one hand, he sees meaning as something highly subjective — every person has to find the unique meaning for each situation of his life, something he does not share with anyone else. On the other hand, however, he sees meaning as something objective, inherent in a situation, "out there," beyond us, to be reached for. It is a dilemma similar to the one religion faces when it maintains that God is at one and the same time in us and "out there," in heaven. It is an intellectual problem, and will not disturb anyone who has experienced God or is leading a meaningful life. But Frankl has tried, as have other psychologists such as Rudolf Allers and Max Wertheimer, to find an intellectual answer.

One may compare reality with a kind of screen used in some theaters. Any kind of picture can be projected on it, and it becomes a backdrop for the scenes played before it. However, when a light is turned on behind the screen, one can see through onto the stage behind it. Reality is like this screen: blank, neutral, so far as meaning is concerned. We can project our self-fabricated meanings onto it and believe that this is the true picture of life, or we can turn on the light that enables us to look through the screen at the reality and the meanings behind it.

Some of the French existentialists, such as Camus and Sartre, believe that man can produce meanings himself and project them onto the empty screen of life. They use phrases such as "Man invents himself" or "Man projects his values." Frankl disagrees with that view. If this were the case, he says, ideals and values would immediately lose their demand quality; if ideals and values were nothing but man's own projections they would not challenge him to reach out for them, and if reality were merely man's wishful thinking projected at an empty screen, all his life, Frankl points out, would be nothing more than a gigantic Rorschach test where everybody sees some blots which everybody interprets in his own way. In this case, meaning would be nothing but a means of self-expression. Yet, no man who is confronted with meaning or who experiences a value, experiences this in terms of "Oh, this just mirrors my present inner conditions." Frankl sees man as experiencing meanings and values as something demanded of him, not something emerging from his own self. He, too, uses the simile of the yogi trick: Some of the existentialists, he maintains, want to make believe that man can project, can throw his own image into nothingness, and that he then will be able to climb up on this self-projection. But to do this is just as impossible as what the yogi pretends to accomplish.

Reaching Out for Objective Reality

According to Frankl, man has the capacity to see through his subjective perspective and perceive the objective reality behind it. Man looks at the world not as through a kaleidoscope but as through a telescope. Frankl explains the difference as follows: In a kaleidoscope man sees only what he himself has put in, and the pattern depends on how he turns the kaleidoscope. But when man looks through a telescope, he looks beyond his subjective perspective — he looks through it and at an objective world. And this is exactly the meaning of "perspective" — *perspicere* means to "look through." Although everyone looks at the same reality from a different, his subjective, viewpoint — what he sees is the same, and an objective, reality. Frankl presented this idea at the Harvard University Summer School in 1961. He pointed through the seminar classroom window at the Harvard Chapel outside, and told his students: "That chapel out there presents itself from a different perspective to each of you depending on where you sit. If two of you were to claim that you see the chapel in exactly the same way, I would have to tell you that one of you is imagining things. But despite this different and highly subjective perspective, no one will deny that the Harvard Chapel out there is one and the same objective reality."

The same is true when man looks at a situation. Men differ in the interpretation of the meaning inherent in a situation. However, not each interpretation is of equal validity. To Frankl, finding the true meaning in a situation is like finding the right answer in a quiz. Several answers are possible, but only one is right; several interpretations of a situation are possible, but only one is the true one.

In his article "What Is Meant by Meaning" in the Winter 1966 issue of the *Journal of Existentialism* he tells the following episode that illustrates the point: One evening, in the question-and-answer period after a lecture, the moderator helped sort out the questions handed in. Suddenly he eliminated one as "sheer nonsense." He read the question as, "Dr. Frankl, how do you define 600 in your theory?" The question was written in blockprint, and when Frankl looked at it, he saw that it read DR. FRANKL, HOW DO YOU DEFINE GOD IN YOUR THEORY? Frankl considered this episode as an unintentional projective test, all the more remarkable because the moderator, a theologian, had read "600" while Frankl, a neurologist, had read "GOD." The right interpretation was, of course, the one that understood the question the way it had been meant by the person who had asked it. That is why

Frankl offers as a definition: "Meaning is what is meant."

Meant by what? By whom? Who poses life's questions? Society? Lawgivers? Conventions and traditions? God? Life itself? Many people will give many different answers. A theologically inclined person will say that God is asking the questions. A nontheologically inclined person will say that life is asking them, or reality, or the world. In any case, someone or something outside us, beyond us, is doing the asking — it really matters little what name we give to the questioner, just as it was of no consequence to know who had handed in the slip of paper.

The important thing is to realize that a question has been asked and that it requires an answer. According to Frankl, man must realize that he is free to respond, but that this freedom must not be confused with arbitrariness. No one can arbitrarily select any answer that comes to his mind; he must realize that there is only one right answer to the question, and that he is responsible for trying his best to find the right answers to the questions that are asked of him, to interpret correctly the meanings inherent in a situation, or, as Frankl puts it, not to invent meanings but to discover them.

Discovery of the undiscoverable is a typical human preoccupation. It has challenged man for thousands of years, and out of this challenge to millions of individuals has come a wisdom that has been passed on to us in the forms of commandments, rules of behavior, ethical laws, and customs which Frankl terms "values" and which can be a help as well as a risk.

CHAPTER IV

The Value of Values

If men cannot always make history have a meaning, they can always act so that their own lives have one.   ALBERT CAMUS

THE DISTINCTION BETWEEN MEANING and value has been developed by Frankl only gradually. In his early writings he used the two terms together, and often as synonyms, but where he applied them separately, value was the broader concept. In recent years, however, the distinction has become quite sharp: he reserves the word "meaning" for "that which is meant" for the individual in each particular situation of his life. Meaning is unique and personal: no one can arrogate for himself a meaning that is meant for someone else, nor can a person who has missed the meaning of a situation come back later and recover it. Life and its string of meanings keep rolling along. That is the basis for the logotherapeutic tenet that each person is unique — he lives his unique life, has his unique opportunities and potentials, but also his unique shortcomings; he creates his unique relationships with others and accepts his unique tasks; he faces his unique sufferings, experiences his unique guilt feelings, and dies his unique death. For the individual, the search for meanings is highly personal and distinct.

But human situations repeat themselves and a great number of individuals respond to them in the same way. Although each person has to try to find his personal and unique meaning, he can learn from others who were in similar circumstances. In many of the typical life situations, therefore, the unique meanings for many individuals and over a long period of time have been similar enough for universal meanings to develop. According to Frankl's definition, such universal meanings are called "values."

Help from Universal Values

The difference between "unique meanings" and "universal values" was illustrated by an incident in a discussion group on logotherapy. One of the participants, a young lady very active in her church, came to the meeting disturbed because a casual acquaintance, a woman in her fifties, had committed suicide the day before. What upset the young lady was the fact that she had seen the woman just before she had killed herself. The woman had seemed depressed and had talked about her daughter's leaving home to accept a job in Denver. "If I had shown some interest," the lady in our group now reproached herself, "perhaps taken her along to the church party to which I was going, I might have prevented the suicide. This was the task required of me at that moment, but I did not recognize the meaning of the situation." In the discussion that followed, several others recalled similar instances in their lives. An elderly man told how, years ago, he had observed the son of a neighbor shoplifting in a store but had said nothing because he did not want to get involved; the boy later went to prison for a holdup and our group member never forgave himself for having missed the opportunity of talking to the boy's father or the boy himself. Another participant, a man in his forties, sadly said, "When I was a kid I always avoided hugging and kissing my mother. I wish I could do it now but she's dead."

In all those instances, the unique meaning of a situation had been missed and was irrevocably lost. Yet, in each case that meaning could have been found with the help of values, those time-tested rules of behavior. The young lady might have been more attentive to her elderly friend by heeding the old advice to "love thy neighbor." The elderly man might have accepted his responsibility to speak to the boy's father by acting upon his belief in the old virtue of honesty. The son of the unhugged mother may have done well to remember the commandment, "Honor thy father and thy mother." It is true that such guidelines, rules, and commandments were developed for mankind as a whole but under normal circumstances individuals may benefit from them. Frankl has explained their function: They can help decision making in confrontations with everyday-life situations. If a man feels a sudden desire for his neighbor's wife, up springs a little warning light, "Thou shalt not covet . . . ," and the warning light is enforced by the law of the land, the power of the church, and the pressure of society. Universal values may even spare the individual decision making altogether: He simply chooses the action that millions of people have found right in similar circumstances. Such choices are what might be called the "lovelorn column" choices — not based on the individual case (of which the columnist knows only one letter's worth), but on the wisdom of the ages — father knows best, honesty is the best policy, be kind to people, mind your own business, follow etiquette and ground rules, remain a virgin until marriage, don't covet your neighbor's wife. Occasionally, a new piece of wisdom creeps into the columns, the not yet thoroughly tested wisdom of the twentieth century: if you are a woman, don't stand for any nonsense from your husband; and if you differ too much from the norm, see a psychiatrist.

Value Conflicts

Although this general advice is based on values, to surrender personal decision to universal rules may prove costly, resulting in a conflict between two sets of overlapping or contradicting values. Such conflicts may present a challenge to some, but also may lead to neuroses.

As Frankl expressed it graphically, meanings — being unique for each person and each situation — cannot overlap, they are one-dimensional points along a line. Points cannot overlap. Values, however, are areas of agreed-upon meanings, covering many points of individual decisions, and areas — such as two circles — may overlap. Overlapping values may cause the conflict of the conscientious objector torn between the value of his religious pacifistic upbringing and that of patriotism — the love for his country and for a society that values such feelings; they cause the conflict of the young man whose father wants him to take over the family business but who himself feels a commitment to the arts; the conflict of the executive caught between the values of a career and a family; of the politician caught between party loyalty and honesty; a wife between the values of her husband and those of her mother; a child between the differing values of two parents. Value conflicts sometimes break into the open when the overriding reality of some commitment is relaxed. A woman who had married her husband during their college days and put him through college, found only after he had received his Ph.D. that they had different and conflicting values. She was interested in raising her small children, but he was interested in his research — a fact that had been obscured during the time when both had the common goal of getting him his degree. Such value conflicts may explain, at least in part, why so many college marriages break up exactly at the time when the most obvious difficulties seem over. A similar danger period in a marriage comes when the children have grown up. The woman faces the choice of filling her sudden vacuum with values she may have set aside for the sake of bringing up the children and of devoting herself to a husband who, meanwhile, has developed values of his own. The result is restlessness, perhaps neurosis, perhaps divorce.

Frankl never ceases to stress, however, that moral or ethical conflicts or, for that matter, spiritual problems in themselves are no disease. He tells the case of an American diplomat who came to his office after having received psychoanalysis for five years in New York. Frankl asked the patient why he had sought the help of the psychoanalyst. It turned out that the patient was dissatisfied with his career and, particularly, found it difficult to implement the American foreign policy at that time. His analyst had told him to reconcile himself with his father because the American government, as well as his superiors, represented to him father images; therefore, his dissatisfaction with his job and the American foreign policy was caused by his unconscious hatred of his father. The patient had accepted the analyst's interpretation until, as Frankl expressed it, "he finally was unable to see the forest of reality because of the trees of symbols and images." After two interviews with the logotherapist it became clear that the patient's will to meaning was frustrated in his career. He was longing for some other kind of work. There was no reason for the "patient" not to switch careers. When he did, his neurotic symptoms disappeared. "I doubt," Frankl commented, "that this man had any neurosis at all. He needed no psychotherapy, not even logotherapy. Not every conflict *per se* — and that is the lesson of the case — is necessarily neurotic."

Because value conflicts are no disease, logotherapy does not attempt to avoid them. Indeed, conflicts cannot be avoided. Like the search for meaning, they are specifically human phenomena and must be taken as part of human existence. Obviously no human being is able to live without value conflicts because practically everything in our lives causes conflicts, including our upbringing, our relationships to parents and friends, our education, our religion, our society, our work, our marriage, and even therapy. The New Zealand pediatrician Margaret Liley flatly states in her book *The Infant World,* "There is no such thing as a completely untraumatic upbringing." Only in special circumstances will value conflicts lead to neuroses — noögenic neuroses which are caused not by conflicting drives but by conflicting values, and thus are rooted not in the patient's psyche but in his noös. Impotence or frigidity may result on noögenic grounds from conflicts between marital vows and puritan upbringing. Noögenic neuroses will respond to logotherapy which attempts to illuminate the conflict for the patient but carefully refrains from making the decision for him. It is always up to the patient to decide freely, responsibly, and according to his own conscience.

The following case illustrates a noögenic neurosis and the

logotherapist's approach to a cure: A young woman came to
a logotherapist because she was suffering from a severe neurosis and reactive depression. As it turned out, her sickness was
rooted in a conflict between the values of her religion and her
marital vows. According to her upbringing, the religious education of her children was of upmost importance to her; her
atheistic husband was opposed to it. The conflict, in itself,
was human. The result of the conflict, however, was a neurosis. The therapist first used drug treatments to bring immediate relief from the psychophysical *effects* of her moral-noëtic
conflict. Then a therapy was begun that concerned itself with
the *causes* of her neurosis. Here, however, it proved to be impossible to treat her neurosis without discussing questions of
meanings and values. The patient remarked that she could
lead a pleasant life and achieve peace of mind if she would adjust to the values of her husband and the society in which he
moved. Her problem now was to decide whether she should
and could adjust to these values at the price of giving up her
own. But this was precisely what she found impossible to do.
Adjusting to her husband's philosophy of life, she said, would
mean "to sacrifice her own self." She expressly stated, "To
renounce my religious convictions would mean a surrender
of my self." This remark was crucial. Had she not made it,
logotherapy could not have proceeded to suggest a course:
It could have neither encouraged the patient to adjust to her
husband's philosophy of life, nor could it have strengthened
the patient's insistence on her own. But now that she had
expressed the existential commitment of her "self" to religious
values, the therapist explained to her that her neurosis was
the result of an attempt to repress her spiritual aspirations
and that, consequently, her neurosis could not be cured without her being true to her self. The patient recognized that she
need not surrender her religious principles to those of her
husband; but that, for the very sake of maintaining these
religious principles, she should avoid any provocation of her
husband and, at the same time, try to open the door for his
better understanding of her religious convictions.

Logotherapy is very insistent on this point — that it is not the therapist's role to transfer his own philosophy to his patient, and he certainly must not allow the patient to shift the decision onto the physician's shoulders. Logotherapy must make the patient aware of his responsibility for making his own decisions. In this particular case logotherapy helped the patient regain her self-confidence and this, in turn, became instrumental in her ability to persuade her husband to agree to a religious education for her children. As time went on, the religious convictions of the woman deepened, but not in the sense of institutionalized religiosity. She could face her husband's views, and also what she regarded as the super-ficiality of the society in which he moved, with both self-assurance and tolerance.

Hierarchy of Values

Throughout the years during which Frankl has refined his theory of values, he has become doubtful about the assumption that value conflicts are unavoidable. In his recent publication, "What Is Meant by Meaning?" he has put forth the theory that values only seem to overlap or collide if they are considered as circles within a two-dimensional plane. Is it conceivable, he asks, that values actually exist like independent spheres in three-dimensional space, neither touching nor colliding nor overlapping, and that it is only their projections on the two-dimensional plane which overlap? This simile led Frankl to the conclusion that value collisions are the result of disregarding one whole dimension, the dimension in which there is a hierarchy, an order of values. Values are of a higher or lower order, and — as the phenomenologist Max Scheler observed — we make value judgments by preferring one value over another. When we are aware of the hierarchy, the so-called value collisions disappear.

This theory is illustrated by what happened when Frankl and his first wife arrived in the Auschwitz concentration camp and the time came to say goodbye to her. When they were separated he told her with great emphasis, so that she would understand his meaning, "Stay alive at all costs. Go to any length to survive." He had become aware that in this unique situation it was his responsibility to give her his absolution in advance for whatever she might find necessary to preserve her life. She was a beautiful woman and it was possible that an SS officer would become interested in her. This could be her chance to save her life, but she might feel inhibited by the thought of her husband and the marital vows that tied her to him. A conflict was threatening between two values, both based on the oldest rules of Western civilization — the Ten Commandments. One was the commandment not to commit adultery; the other, not to kill. For Frankl felt that by not releasing his wife from her moral obligations toward him he might become co-responsible for her death. He might have indirectly contributed to her being killed, as he expressed it later, "for the sake of a husband's narcissism if I had placed the commandment not to commit adultery above the one not to kill." But, he explained, a theologian could evade the dilemma by pointing out that the commandment forbidding adultery is not supreme. "There is a hierarchy even within the Ten Commandments, one could argue," Frankl observed. "The commandments have been numbered from one to ten, but this numerical order does not imply a ranking of values. Each individual must find the rank of the commandments as the specific situation demands it. What I did in Auschwitz," he said, "was to respond to a unique situation. I found the specific meaning of this unique situation — and I found that it contradicted a widely accepted value. But I distinctly felt that it was the requirement of the moment to give my absolution in advance — a requirement, to be sure, that might have been valid neither before nor after this situation. For I do hope that saying goodbye in Auschwitz is a situation that will not occur again."

Man constantly is confronted with apparent value conflicts. Life is a string of decisions that must be based on value judgments, decisions between seemingly conflicting values, and decisions about meanings in specific situations. Most decisions concern prosaic, everyday conflicts. On a Sunday morning, shall I go to church, go fishing, spend the day with my family, sleep? What shall I do with some windfall money — take a vacation, have the roof of my house repaired, save it, give it to charity? Seen in this light, there would be no such thing as having no time or no money — it simply is a matter of giving rank and values. Having no time for a certain activity means that one wishes to save the time for other activities one considers more essential.

In a seminar, Frankl gave this example of simple value conflicts in his own daily activities: "On a certain morning, should I devote myself to my family or look up a patient at the hospital? Actually, this is no conflict when I can see that the value of my professional visit, in the service of mankind, is of a higher order than just sitting with my wife and my daughter. But suppose my wife needs me because she is sick. Then the choice seems to be one sick person against another. But there is a difference because in one case I am replaceable, and in the other I am not. In the case of my patient at the hospital I can send a member of my staff to look after him." The questions "Who is replaceable?" and "Who is unique in this situation?" carry great weight in deciding value conflicts. "If someone," said Frankl, "rings me up and wants an appointment with me, I first ask him who recommended me as a doctor. If he says, 'A friend told me,' or 'Another doctor mentioned your name,' I am likely to refer him to a member of my staff. But when he says, 'I heard you speak on the radio ten years ago and I trust only you,' I'll make every effort to see him myself, even if he cannot pay a fee. For this is a unique obligation and I am relatively irreplaceable. Or another example: Shall I expand my private practice, or spend more time teaching seminars? See more patients in person or let my staff see them, and use the time I save to write a book? We have to see where we have a unique obligation and where we can be replaced by others."

Thus, the decision again is returned to the individual. Even though general values help the individual in his decision making, he still must decide about the rank of conflicting — or seemingly conflicting — values, and he also must decide on occasion to take a stand against a value if he feels the situation demands it. It is an important point in logotherapy to realize that value hierarchy, like meaning, cannot be arbitrarily fabricated. It must be found by personal effort. It won't do to project our own order of values on the empty screen of life; we must illuminate the reality behind the screen. Whether it is placed there by God or by life is a question each person must decide for himself. The important thing to realize is that a value hierarchy exists and that it is up to each person to find it.

To arbitrarily establish such a hierarchy is dangerous. Even high and universally accepted values must not be arbitrarily elevated onto a pedestal and worshiped out of all proportion to other values. This is idolatry, and Frankl insists that every idolatry carries its own punishment by leading to despair. And by the same token, every despair is based, in the last analysis, on idolatry of one value above all others. He quotes his teacher Rudolf Allers as saying that idolatry destroys the idol worshiper exactly in that area where he sinned against the value hierarchy. In Hitler Germany, the values of "blood and soil" were raised to the status of an idol and all other values were subordinated. As a result, Germany lost exactly that — blood and soil: the blood of her young generation and large parts of her territory.

No one, neither the state nor the psychiatrist, can determine for others what their meanings and value hierarchy should be. What the psychiatrist can do, and what the logotherapist emphasizes, is to help the individual see that he has the capacity to discover meanings and among values a hierarchy, and to point to man's conscience as the instrument with which he can make his existential decisions.

CHAPTER V

Our Intuitive Conscience

Conscience is as much a part of man as his leg or arm.
THOMAS JEFFERSON

How we mortals are to know the "will of God," those never-promulgated laws of the ultimate Lawgiver, has remained one of man's unanswered and probably unanswerable questions. As Frankl once said, with reference to the ultimate meaning of life, the only answers that really can be given are the one given by Job (that we do not know it) and the one given by Socrates (that the only thing we do know is that we know nothing). Nor do the answers come more easily when the question is asked in terms of logotherapy: How can we know the meaning of a situation? Occasionally, a situation allows rational man to find a rational answer. In the anecdote of "the meaning of 600," it was easy to see, once the alternatives were raised, that GOD and not 600 had been "meant" by the person who asked the question. In the questions raised by life, however, we do not always see the alternatives and, if we do, the right answer is not obvious. This is so because life's questions frequently allow no rational answers. As Frankl sees it, the meaning of a situation is unique, it does not fall under a general law, and therefore rational thinking alone is no help in our search for meaning. Nor can we depend on our instincts as animals can. Having lost most of his instinctual directives, and finding reason of little help, man must turn to the intuitive voice of his conscience.

Rediscovery of Conscience

To proclaim our conscience as the apt guide for our behavior, as logotherapy does, certainly is nothing new. It is, phrased in twentieth-century terminology, man's oldest answer to one of his oldest questions. Rather than a discovery, it is a rediscovery, but one that is vital at this point in history. In Frankl's existential concept of man one may see a modern rephrasing of Biblical images. According to the Biblical concepts, man is a creature made from earth but graced with God's own breath. He is a physical shape but is also spiritual. Man has eaten from the Tree of Knowledge and is able to distinguish Good from Evil, but at the price of expulsion from Paradise. Here we are, then, laboring by the sweat of our brow, but possessing the cursed and blessed godlike freedom to make choices. Since Biblical times, and until fairly recently, we accepted the idea that something within us was godlike (even if it was "stolen" from God and perhaps has been the reason for much of our suffering) and that our conscience was the voice of God speaking from our depth and reaching out to the highest.

In recent times, however, "conscience" has become the victim of reductionist thinking. Because it could not be researched in the physical and psychological dimensions of man, it has been widely discarded as a true part of the human makeup: scientific man is inclined to see our conscience as nothing but the outcome of conditioning processes, or to consider it in terms of a superego. Under such an interpretation, man acts "moral" because he is trained in a certain way or because he is complying with his father image. In this way, the noëtic phenomenon called conscience — and in logotherapy, noëtic means distinctly human — has been degraded to a subhuman level. Frankl rejects such interpretations as reductionist explanations; indeed, he defines reductionism as "subhumanism." Conscience, on the other hand, he sees as a distinctly human phenomenon, not the mere consequence of training, father images, or anything else, but something primary and primordial. Accordingly, he defines conscience as our intuitive capacity to find out, to "sniff out," the unique meaning *gestalt* inherent in a situation, to tell us "what is meant" in a specific situation.

Conscience is an exclusively human quality not shared by

any other creature. A story Frankl tells in his lectures concerns the dog that has soiled the carpet and slinks under the couch. This, he says, is not conscience but "anticipatory anxiety," a fear of getting punished, the result of conditioning. Man's conscience must not be reduced to such a level. And neither must conscience be regarded in terms of a superego because that would presuppose that man is moral only because he wants to be at peace with his father image, or to quiet his discontented superego. Frankl calls this pseudomorality. Such a view, he says, misses the point of true morality, which begins only when man has decided to act for the sake of a cause, a person, or a deity, not for his own sake, nor to have a clear conscience or to get rid of the stimulus of a discontented superego.

Frankl's interpretation takes conscience at its face value, as something originally human, and not merely the result of environment, conditioning, or impulses.

In such an interpretation he is not alone among contemporary psychologists. For instance, Gerhard Adler, a follower of Carl Jung, in *Studies in Analytical Psychology* defines conscience as "our inner moral and ethical laws, our inner voice, or whatever else one may like to call these formative factors," and states that these "are due to an a priori condition of the human psyche — they are manifestations of the self."

A Phenomenological Approach

Frankl's concepts, however, are more sharply defined because he has always been a man of strict methodology. To analyze human experience he uses the phenomenological method of Husserl and Scheler, which is also the basis of Heidegger's existential philosophy. Frankl defines the phenomenological method as an approach that describes the actual way in which we experience the world and ourselves, but without fitting the phenomena of our experiences into preconceived patterns of interpretation — as we do when we do not take hu-

man phenomena at their face value but reduce them to a subhuman level. An example of a preconceived pattern of interpretation is the a priori assumption that values can be nothing
but defense mechanisms and reaction formations, conscience
nothing but superego, love nothing but sex. If we thus ex-
clude in advance all humanness from the human dimension,
we shall never be able to find man but only the animal, perhaps only the computer.

As he frequently does, Frankl illustrates this philosophical
concept with a Jewish joke: Two men seek a rabbi's judgment.
The first claims that the other's cat has eaten his butter. The
second denies this. The rabbi asks the first man how much
butter the cat has eaten. "Two pounds," answers the man.
The rabbi weighs the cat and finds it weighs two pounds.
"Now we have found the butter," decides the rabbi, "but
where is the cat?" The rabbi disputed away the objective
reality of the cat, for the sake of a preconceived assumption
that if there are two pounds, they must be butter.

The phenomenological method stresses reality as we experience and observe it — reality as it is really lived by the
man in the street, or in the concentration camp, in the executive offices, or in the loneliness of his room; a reality not
reduced to satisfy some a priori assumptions. In this sense of
an all-inclusive concept of reality, conscience, the centerpiece
of the noëtic dimension, is as much a part of reality as man's
body and his psyche. To really understand Frankl, we must
remember that science first explored only the physical dimension of man and later the psychological. The spirit had
no place in this scientific concern with the reality of material
things. Religion, on the other hand, has always emphasized
the spirit, to the extent of tending to downgrade the body as
evil, shameful, and a burden to man's attainment of eternal
life. Both science and religion are likely to forget that these
theoretical concepts are merely ways in which man can *think*
about his existence, but that in his *actual* existence man is
not a body, a psyche, nor a noös but an indivisible unit,
man. Frankl feels that this concept of an indivisible man in

the face of the growing pluralism of scientific thought is the most important topic of this age. He selected this theme in his address to the world elite of scholars at the 600th anniversary of the University of Vienna in 1965, where he was the only commemorative speaker from the field of medicine who had been selected to give a scientific lecture. He chose for its title "The Pluralism of Sciences and the Unity of Man."

Conscience is reality. True conscience is not just what father, or religion, or society tells us. All these forces are indeed real, but at the core of ourselves we still have this strange little device. It plays a central part in our lives: how we listen and how we act upon what we have heard can make our life either meaningful or empty; it can cause happiness and fulfillment, or tension, conflicts, frustration, and mental disease.

Our Task to Listen

The rediscovery by existential logotherapy of an authentic human conscience has a number of practical consequences. One of these is our task to listen. We need to respond to a task so that we may lead a meaningful life. It may not be wrong to assume that our central task is to listen to our conscience. We act as humans only if we act because we have decided to, and not because we are driven to it or because we are afraid of punishment. It is true that commandments and laws threaten punishment, but so long as man lives according to them automatically, he has ruled himself out as a person, a self. The Ten Commandments are among the best guidelines we have, but merely following them is not enough; as Frankl points out, we have to find out for ourselves the unique meanings from many more than just ten — from ten thousand, ten million — individual situations with which we are confronted. In each case we have to listen to our conscience which, on occasion (as in the example of Frankl's saying goodbye to his wife in the concentration camp), may even advise us to go contrary to one of the Ten Commandments. Many people have felt that without our conscience we should have only rules to go by, and rules won't always work because they are general and may become outdated. Mere rules, as Americans will be the first to admit, tend to suffocate us unless we accept them by our own free will. But free will must be used responsibly and not merely arbitrarily. We have the task to listen to our inner ear, which can pick up whispers about ultimate meanings and a hierarchy of values otherwise inaccessible. The imagery has changed significantly: In Biblical times man behaved morally for fear of an eye in the sky; today, because he has decided to respond to what he hears with his inner ear. The eye in the sky was a threat from the outside and inescapable, but it is up to us to decide whether to pay attention to our inner ear, and we can turn it off if we wish. We are free to move with or against our spiritual pull. Man can be browbeaten, persuaded, hypnotized, brainwashed, or shamed into honoring his father and mother, but the human way is free choice.

Thus we have the task of listening to the voice of our conscience which, in turn, is our individual listening post to ideals and values and challenges. But we take a tremendous risk by following our conscience. Frankl is careful to point out that our conscience, being genuinely human, also has that typically human quality, the ability to err: "It can not only guide us, it may mislead us. Even more, we never know, not even on our deathbed, whether it has been the true meaning to which we committed ourselves. But although our conscience may err, we have to obey it. The possibility of error does not release us from the necessity of trying." The thought that we have to risk error was also forcefully expressed by Gordon W. Allport, professor of psychology at Harvard University: "We can be at one and the same time half-sure and whole-hearted."[1]

Conscience in Hitler Germany

Even greater than the risk of an erring conscience is the risk of suppressing the voice of conscience altogether. Under drastic circumstances it may make someone an Eichmann or a

Hitler. Frankl often is asked about the conscience of the Germans under National Socialism: did it tell them to betray their fathers and mothers for the sake of the state, to plunder Jewish stores, and commit mass murder? Frankl's answer is that he does not believe that Hitler ever obeyed his conscience. Never can one's true conscience, he says, command a man to do what Hitler did. "If Hitler had really listened to the voice of his conscience, he would not have become Hitler."

Hitler's Germany also illustrates what can happen if conscience becomes the result of a mere indoctrination by a dictatorship. In Hitler's Reich conscience was conditioned along the lines of the myth of a superrace. The tragedy of the Germans was exactly that they mistook the dictates of the state for the voice of conscience. If they had listened to their individual consciences, they would have been able to decide whether they wanted to follow the demand of their conscience or that of their society. And there were some who did follow the voice of their conscience, dangerous though this was in the times of the Third Reich. Rabbi Harold Schulweis of Oakland, California, several years ago founded the "Institute for the Righteous Acts," devoted to finding German citizens who risked their lives to help and hide Jews and other victims of the Nazi regime. The Institute has found a number of such "righteous men," some martyred by the Nazis, some still alive. Frankl himself knows of some who, following the dictates of their conscience, joined the resistance movement, were imprisoned in concentration camps, and died there. On his lecture tours in the United States he is sometimes asked why he returned to Vienna after his own concentration camp experiences. He then points to the Catholic Baroness who, at great peril, hid one of Frankl's cousins during the war years, or to the socialist attorney whom he had known only slightly, but who supplied him with potatoes and tomatoes in 1942 when food was severely rationed and any contact with Jews was dangerous. These were exceptions, to be sure, but so were the murderers and robbers. The concept of collective guilt is rejected by Frankl. But if there was "guilt" at all with the majority, it was the "crime" of remaining passive, of having heard but not acted upon the voice of their conscience. He occasionally mentions such cases as that of a well-known Viennese actress, who had been forced by Hitler's minister, Josef Goebbels, to accept the lead in a Nazi propaganda movie. Many people later expressed the view that she should have refused, and have risked being sent to a concentration camp rather than lend prestige and popularity to the Hitler cause. In principle, Frankl agrees; but, he feels, such extreme heroism can be demanded only by those who proved by their own action that they made the choice of going to a concentration camp rather than to collaborate. And he observes that actual survivors of the camps tend to be more tolerant than others because they know the full import of such a decision.

Frankl often concludes such discussions on Hitlerism with the observation that he prefers living in a world in which man is challenged to choose his own existence; a world, that is, in which such phenomena as Hitler and a saint can coexist. He prefers such a world to one in which there is nothing but complete conformism and collectivism, where everyone is forced to act in a certain way, either by a state or a party.

The Risk of Uncertainty

The voice of conscience speaks to us, but we are free to say NO. This is our choice: To listen and follow as best we can, or to surrender our freedom and consider ourselves driven by forces beyond our control.

Thus we are not determined by conscience, but led by it. Sometimes, however, Frankl adds, we may also be misled by it. This is another consequence of the rediscovery of a highly personal conscience: the awareness that we must make our choices in the face of ultimate uncertainty. This has always been difficult for man to accept. People want certainty and, because they cannot make their own decisions with assurance, they have been clinging to divine pronouncements, dogmas, axioms, canons, commandments, laws, and principles. Religious man finds certainty in the word of God as it becomes accessible through sacred books and holy men. Scientific man had high hopes that because he found order in the physical universe, he eventually should find certainty and order in life. But such hopes have not been sustained. Science has disproved man's belief that the more he knows the less is left to know. The telescope only showed us the vastness of our ignorance. Our universe is expanding, and it is possible that certainty is flying apart as fast as the galaxies. We may have to face the possibility that, even in the physical world, man forever lives on the edge of the unknown. As Blaise Pascal said, the more the sphere of science is extended, the more the unknown comes in contact with its surface. Even the natural scientist who deals with measurable material cannot wait until all the evidence is in; he has to start with assumptions, deal with relationships, and commit himself to findings based on uncertainty. We cannot hope to do better in our daily lives. We have to live existentially, without first attempting to understand the entire system on which life is based. But even without understanding fully, we can make our assumptions, form relationships, and accept commitments, and, based on such expectations, live a meaningful life. The faith needed in such a life is not a faith that conforms to dogmas and laws, but a faith that transforms us into beings with better relationships and higher commitments.

To face the possibility that we may have to lead a life of eternal uncertainty, with no readily accessible authority to turn to but our feeble conscience, may be a principal cause of our present anxiety. We live in a period of history when people — not just a few isolated individuals, but a sizable number — are beginning to realize that the belief in ultimate certainty may be an illusion, and that we have to accept uncertainty as a precondition of humanity. We may have to accept the uncertainties of life and death, the uncertainties of knowledge and conduct. We may have to accept the possibility that, although order and certainty and ultimate meaning must be taken as axioms of our existence, and life without them is unthinkable, we may not have the capacity to grasp universal order and meaning on our human level, and that the only way to have glimpses of them is through our intuitive but possibly erring conscience. We have to face the fact that we must constantly make our decisions on the basis of incomplete evidence. Columbus never would have discovered America had he waited for all the information on which to base his decision to start out on his journey. And few people would decide on a career, marriage, or parenthood if they waited until all the information was in. We must constantly venture out in a sea of uncertainty. Frankl's thesis is that, although we are uncertain about guidance by our conscience, we have no choice but to venture and follow its voice. And he adds that we not only need the spirit of venture in our uncertainty, but also the quality of tolerance. Because we can never be certain whether our conscience has shown us the right way in a specific situation, we can never be certain whether our conscience or that of another person was right. That is why we must be tolerant of the conduct of others, and above all, we must acknowledge that others may obey the voice of their conscience as they hear it. This attitude, Frankl warned, must not lead to indifference, only to tolerance: "Indifference would mean that everybody is equally right. This is nonsense. Objectively, there can be only one right answer, one true meaning to a situation; but we cannot know whether we have been able to grasp it — perhaps someone else did while we failed. Therefore, we must be tolerant. However, this does not at all mean that I share a belief with someone else — it only means that I regard him as a human being with equal rights to stick to his own convictions."

The Presence of Conflicts

Another consequence of this concept of conscience is the unavoidable presence of conflicts. If our conscience can say NO to God, commandments, laws, government, society, inner drives, parents, spouses, our upbringing, and our past, then conflicts are unavoidable. Every moment brings choice, every choice brings conflicts, and every conflict brings tension. To Frankl (and this is discussed more fully in the next chapter) tensions are inherent in the human condition; tensions between what a man is and what his conscience tells him he ought to be; between his reality and his ideals. To reduce this kind of tension would rob him of his humanness. Tension can sharpen man's conscience — a guilty conscience can be a gift from heaven if it leads to a higher self-criticism, better self-understanding, and final "self-improvement," to quote the title of a book by Rudolf Allers, one of Frankl's most revered teachers.

One does not need to be around Frankl very long before becoming aware that he is listening to his conscience very attentively, sometimes with surprising results. After a lecture in Palo Alto, California, he was told that a prisoner in San Quentin had read his book, *Man's Search for Meaning,* and that it had changed his entire outlook on life. The director of San Quentin had heard that Frankl was in the area — would it be possible for him to see the prisoner? To the consternation of all those who had helped arrange his California trip, Frankl reshuffled the entire schedule of the next day, to allow for the visit to San Quentin. Another time, a film company in Hollywood offered him cash for a movie option on his book. He insisted on seeing some of the company's productions (which were full of violence and sensationalism) and refused the offer. Sometimes he can be rude in compliance with his conscience. On his American lecture tours he almost always refuses dinner invitations or even short chats over cups of coffee because he feels that working on a lecture, or simply resting in preparation for a lecture, is more important to his life task than social obligations. (The European style of social life allows for more privacy.) But then again he can be extremely tolerant of the conscience of someone else. When I was in Vienna (after an absence of 27 years), he set aside an

evening to give me an added opportunity to ask him specific
questions. The date conflicted with a Burgtheater performance of a play I had wanted to see (and he knew how I missed
the Vienna theater in the United States). I felt embarrassed
to cancel our interview in favor of a play, but he immediately
agreed, facetiously using his own terminology: "This is the
only time this play is being shown during your stay here.
This is a unique opportunity; for you this is the meaning of
the situation. We can have the talk tomorrow."

Logotherapeutic Dream Interpretation

But conflicts of conscience may have serious consequences
and, in some instances, lead to noögenic neuroses. Neuroses
rooted in conscience conflicts — just as those based on value
collisions — originate in the noëtic part of our unconscious,
the part into which we have repressed, not our drives, but the
advice of our conscience. The logotherapist will help his patient make conscious his unconscious spirituality and morality, just as the psychoanalyst attempts to make conscious the
patient's unconscious drives. For instance, the logotherapist
will help the patient make conscious his unconscious longing
for a higher, or even the ultimate, meaning of his life — his
repressed will to meaning — or the repressed voice of his conscience. Like the repressed drives, the repressed voice of the
conscience will sometimes reveal itself in dreams. The psychoanalyst looks to dreams for manifestations of the instinctual
unconscious; the logotherapist looks for telltale signs from the
spiritual unconscious. Therefore, logotherapy in principle
uses free associations for dream interpretation. As Frankl likes
to express this relationship between the two schools of therapy, "We march together, but we fight different battles."

The conscience of the patient may use dreams to warn
him of dangers which he does not see in his wakeful state, or
to confront him with self-criticism, which he does not face
consciously. An example for each is presented by Frankl in
his book, *Der Unbewusste Gott* (The Unconscious God), not
yet available in English. A woman dreamed that she took her

dirty wash to the laundry, including a dirty cat. When she picked up the clean laundry again, the cat was dead. In discussing the dream, the patient said that she loved cats. She also loved her 23-year-old daughter, her only child. The mother admitted that she worried about the gossip surrounding her daughter's love life — her "dirty linen" was washed in public. The cat therefore stood for her daughter. The dirtiness of the cat signified the moral conduct of the girl, which had come under suspicion. The patient had constantly watched and hounded her daughter because of her suspected "immorality." The dream, therefore, expressed a warning by the patient's conscience not to torment her daughter with exaggerated demands of moral "cleanliness" — or she might lose her child.

The other example, from the same book, illustrated how a dream can voice a self-reproach that is not admitted to the conscious level. A successful composer of popular music sought Frankl's help. The clue to the case came through a dream. The patient had dreamed he was in another city and wanted to phone a certain lady. But the dial was so complex that he could not make the connection. After waking, the patient realized that the number he meant to dial was not the lady's but that of a record company for which he was then working. In a logotherapeutic interpretation of the dream, it turned out that the patient had no romantic interest in the lady, but had spent a happy summer in that city composing serious music. The dream, therefore, was interpreted as dealing not with repressed sex desire rooted in the psychological unconscious, but as a conflict of the artistic conscience in the realm of the noëtic: it reminded the artist-patient that he had a difficult choice (represented by a complex dial) between retaining a well-paying, humdrum job as a composer of hits, or becoming a writer of serious music. This was an existential problem — a question as to the direction in which he wanted to go. It was this decision that had been too painful to be faced openly. Thus the analysis of the dream revealed an existential rather than a sexual frustration.

A Voice from the Unconscious

To consider conscience as an intuitive force within us has the
further consequence that our conscience can show us truth
where it is inaccessible to our rational approach. In a way, all
our important existential decisions are basically intuitive,
and sometimes we justify them by rationalizing them later.
An illustration is found in the story Frankl told at the Conference on Existential Psychiatry, in Toronto, 1962. It is
quoted here from *Psychotherapy and Existentialism,* pages
34–35:

> Shortly before the United States entered World War II,
> I was called to the American Consulate in Vienna to receive
> my immigration visa. My old parents expected me to leave
> Austria as soon as the visa was given. However, at the last
> moment I hesitated: The question of whether I should leave
> my parents beset me. I knew that any day they could be
> taken to a concentration camp. Shouldn't I stay with them?
> While pondering this question I found that this was the type
> of dilemma which made one wish for a hint from Heaven. It
> was then that I noticed a piece of marble lying on a table at
> home. When I asked my father about it, he explained that he
> had found it on the site where the National Socialists had
> burned down the largest Viennese synagogue. My father had
> taken this marble piece home because it was a part of the
> tablets which contained the Ten Commandments. The piece
> showed one engraved and gilded Hebrew letter. My father
> explained that this letter was the abbreviation for only one
> of the Commandments. Eagerly I asked, "Which one is it?"
> The answer was: "Honor thy father and thy mother: that thy
> days may be long upon the land." So I stayed with my father
> and my mother upon the land and decided to let the Ameri-
> can visa lapse.
>
> Acknowledging this piece of marble as a hint from Heaven
> might well be the expression of the fact that already long
> before, in the depth of my heart, I had decided to stay. I
> only projected this decision into the appearance of the mar-
> ble piece. Much the same way would it be self-expression if

one saw nothing but $CaCO_3$ in it — although I would call this rather a projection of an existential vacuum . . .

Whether Frankl's decision was right he will never know; one may argue that it was a futile gesture, or that it helped him to become the human being he now is. The intuitive quality of conscience always points beyond reason into a dimension where reality changes by the very fact of our decision.

In one respect, Frankl says, our conscience is like love: love lets us see the potentialities of the beloved person that have not yet been actualized. These potentialities are unique. And whatever is unique eludes the grasp of pure reason — we can only seize it by intuition. Similarly, conscience makes us aware of the meaning potentials of a situation not yet actualized, thus making reality out of what might otherwise have remained an unfulfilled possibility.

An Instrument of Human Progress

This interpretation of conscience as a personal, intuitive out-· reach into the world of unique meaning potentialities makes it ultimately the instrument of human progress. Conscience is that quality in man that stands up to authority, law, society, and all outside influences, and sees something fresh behind old truths. It's a long way from a society that accepted cannibalism as moral (and probably of religious significance), to one in which young people risk social ostracism for refusing to kill even enemies in war. One can imagine a father in a primitive tribe telling his son who refused to eat the flesh of other human beings: "Don't sin against God. He wouldn't have made people out of flesh if he had not wanted us to eat them." Yet, the son refused. Frankl, in discussing such a hypothetical incident, declared: "In a society that universally accepted cannibalism, only a person with an exceedingly refined conscience could have been able to contradict the environment in which he was brought up. When that person's conscience contradicted cannibalism, he became a revolutionary. He may have been killed, but he was able to awaken the conscience of others. This is the way human progress takes place. And in particular, this is the way revolutions are started — and religions are founded."

Admittedly, progress is desperately slow as measured in one person's life. People take a long time to act according to what they know is right. Most signers of the Declaration of Independence, which named liberty among man's inalienable rights, owned slaves. The mills of conscience, one might say, grind exceedingly slowly, and it is often impossible to decide, for a long time, whether they produce wheat or chaff. What of all these movements of today that are based on the conscience of individuals — the fights against segregation, the student sit-ins, the peace marches, the sexual freedom fights, the rebellion against parental authority, the resistance against too much governmental power, the upsurge of black power and white backlash — are all these movements spurred on by true or deceived consciences? Frankl shrugs off such questions. Only history will be able to tell. At present, none of the persons involved can know for certain whether he is a sound revolutionary or just a nonconformist defying society. Yet, he has to follow his conscience the best he can, keep sharpening his ear to hear its voice, and try to be tolerant toward the actions of others who after all are also following their consciences. This is not easily done in our age of science, when human progress is measured in data that can be counted, calculated, fed into computers, and analyzed. But the answers we get in return from the computers can only tell us how man behaves on the average and in sample groups, never how the individual ought to behave in specific situations. Our life is not regulated, at every crossing, by a red light that tells us to stop, or a green light that tells us to go ahead. We live in an era of the flashing yellow light, leaving the decision to the individual.

CHAPTER VI

The Pursuit of Meaning

*The indefatigable pursuit of an unattainable perfection . . .
is what alone gives meaning to our life.*

LOGAN PEARSALL SMITH

IN LOGOTHERAPY, THE PURSUIT OF MEANING is more than man's
inalienable right — it is the essence of his humanness. If he
represses it, he opens up in himself the infernal pit of the
existential vacuum. If he devotes himself to this pursuit, his
life is filled, not only with meaning but also with the by-products of a meaningful existence — and among these are happiness, security, peace of mind, mental stability, and such
currently fashionable life goals as self-actualization and peak
experiences. All these, Frankl claims, will elude man if he
consciously sets out to gain them, while they will fall into his
lap as the unintended results of his search for meaning. These
best things in life are not exactly free — their price is the acceptance of man's responsibility to find out from moment to
moment what life demands of him individually.

Pursuit of Happiness a Self-Contradiction

These consequences of man's pursuit of meaning follow from
logotherapy's basic belief that man is not a closed system, but
that he reaches out, beyond himself, "into a world full of
fellow beings to encounter and meanings to fulfill," as Frankl
puts it. "These beings and meanings provide man with a
reason to be happy. Happiness *en*sues if he has a reason to be
happy. If, on the other hand, he *pur*sues happiness, it becomes the objective of his motivation and, even worse, the
object of his attention. To the degree to which this takes
place he no longer can be happy. I am sorry to say but the

pursuit of happiness amounts to a self-contradiction: the more
we pursue it the less we attain it."

In an article, "Beyond Self-Expression and Self-Actualization," published in the first issue of the first volume of the
Journal of Existential Psychiatry, Frankl illustrates by analogous phenomena the self-defeating character of happiness
intentionally pursued. Sleep, for instance, will not come by
pursuing it directly — a direct effort to fall asleep will make
the person only tense and sleepless. Good health will not
come to the man overconcerned with it — he has already
fallen sick with hypochondria. Prestige will be denied to
those who are too much occupied with it — they will meet
contempt as status seekers. Good conscience, as mentioned,
will not be awarded to the person who acts in order to have
a good conscience but to him who does his deeds for their
own sake — the good conscience comes as a by-product.

The fact that man will miss pleasure when he makes it his
target, Frankl also demonstrates through cases of sexual
neurosis. Perhaps as much as 90 percent of sexual neurosis,
according to his findings, can be traced to the male's intent
to demonstrate his potency and the female's intent to demonstrate her ability to experience orgasm. They concentrate on
themselves instead of on their partners whom they love.
Frankl believes that this pursuit of sexual happiness, this
direct attempt to experience pleasure, dooms it to failure.
Logotherapy has developed a technique of de-reflection, by
which the patient is helped to shift the focus of his attention
away from himself. (This technique is discussed briefly in
Chapter IX and more fully in Frankl's *The Doctor and the
Soul.*) Frankl found this same principle true not only for
sexual pleasure seeking but for happiness in general. What
we really want, he maintains, is not happiness but reasons to
be happy and partners to make us happy; "however, as soon
as happiness moves to the center of our attention, we lose
sight of the reasons and partners — in other words, of the
possible causes of our happiness — and consequently, happi-

ness disappears." Our intent to be happy, one might say, is crowding out the reasons that would make us happy, and thus the intentional pursuit of happiness proves self-defeating.

I experienced this self-defeating nature of happiness intentionally pursued when, on my first visit to the Alps after an absence of 27 years, I tried to recapture the happiness I had felt in my youth, hiking in the mountains filled with wild flowers and the song of birds. I joined a hiking group, led by a naturalist, going to my favorite mountain area. We were walking single file, constantly looking out for rare specimens. Every few moments the naturalist would stop at a flower, gather the entire group around him, and lecture. Or he would tiptoe to a tree, forefinger on lips, pointing to a bird on a branch. I learned much about birds and flowers but could not recapture that feeling of utmost joy that had filled me on those previous hikes which I had taken merely for the sake of experiencing the beauty of nature. It was a case of one bird in the hand being worth less than two left singing in the bushes.

Happiness, too, is best enjoyed when left in the bushes while we walk the path of life. From Aristotle to Jefferson, happiness has been regarded as the principal goal of life, and its pursuit central to human existence. But such philosophers as Immanuel Kant and Max Scheler warned that pleasure was not an aim but a side effect. Freud made man's pleasure principle a central force of human motivation, but Frankl sides with Kant and Scheler, adding that pleasure establishes itself automatically when we fulfill a meaning or realize a value. The feelings of happiness, pleasure, and peak experience are always the same, even though the reasons may differ widely. But, as Frankl points out, no one can isolate happiness from its reasons. To make this statement clearer, he quotes Abraham Maslow's sentence, "In the real world there is no such thing as blushing without something to blush about."[1] Only in a context, Maslow says, is blushing possible; similarly, Frankl adds, only in a context is happiness possible — the context of a reason to be happy. A person cannot find a relationship with happiness itself, only with actions and people giving him happiness.

Casual students of logotherapy sometimes object to the idea that happiness comes only in response to a task. Happiness, they say, comes and goes as it pleases, and often at the most unexpected moments — while walking alone in a thunderstorm, or watching the waves break against rocks, or lying in a meadow with a beloved person. These critics overlook the thesis of logotherapy that meaning, and happiness, can come not only as a by-product of some activity, or "task" in a narrow sense, but also as the result of an experience, be it aesthetic, intellectual, or emotional. After all, one of the three categories of values, as Frankl distinguishes them, are those "experiential values" which are realized whenever we enjoy nature or culture, and whenever we experience beauty, truth, and goodness in the world.

Reasons and Causes for Happiness

In Berkeley, where interest in the pursuit of happiness via psychedelic drugs is high, Frankl was asked what he thought about inducing pleasure and peak experiences by artificial means, such as LSD, "happiness pills," or alcohol. His answer:

> Alcohol and drugs can, of course, never be a "reason" for happiness, but they may be a cause. Reason implies a psychological relationship, but cause is strictly physiological. When I am weeping because I lost a friend, I have a reason; but when I am weeping while cutting an onion, the onion is not a reason for my tears — it is a cause. Happiness, too, can be induced by a cause — by pills and even an electric current. I know of an experiment, where electrodes were implanted in a certain spot in the brains of rats, and every time a rat pushed a lever, apparently the animal experienced sexual pleasure or the pleasure resulting from food intake. The rats eventually pressed the lever thousands of times a day and neglected the real food and their real sex partner. That is the way people behave who use causes rather than

reasons to experience pleasure. The causes may well be chemical but the reasons must be human.

Psychedelic drugs, Frankl suspects, may be popular today because people, not being able to find reasons for happiness in the objective world around them, are looking for causes which they can fabricate themselves. He illustrated that point with a joke he had found in the *American Journal of Psychotherapy*. A deaf patient is told by his doctor to stop drinking whiskey. Two months later he is cured of deafness, but at the next visit the patient is as deaf as before: he is drinking again. "You see," he explains to his doctor, "first I drank and didn't hear. Then I quit drinking and heard. But frankly, Doctor, *what* I heard was not as good as whiskey." Similarly, people who can see no meanings beckoning them from the outside that are worth pursuing, withdraw to the self-fabricated peak experiences of the psychedelic drugs. They are trying to fill their existential vacuum.

As a therapeutic tool, however, psychedelics — like other drugs — may be useful in connection with logotherapy. Frankl sees possible usefulness for LSD in its ability, revealed by medical research, to produce in patients a mental state in which thoughts and feelings assume an exaggerated sense of meaning. There are scientific reports to the effect that under the influence of psychedelics, patients seem to have prolonged experiences that help them see old ideas in a new light and make them accept new ideas more readily.

Self-Actualization

Self-actualization — another concept which, along with peak experiences, has become popular through modern psychological literature — is desirable but also can be achieved only to the extent to which a person fulfills the concrete meaning of a specific life situation. If he seeks self-actualization for its own sake, he will miss his aim. To stress this favorite point of his, Frankl quotes two men, living 2,500 years apart: the ancient Greek poet Pindar, who admonished man, in one of the earliest samples of existential advice, to "become what he is," but also the contemporary existentialist Karl Jaspers, who supplements Pindar by stating, "What man is he has become through that cause which he has made his own."

In his article on self-actualization mentioned before, Frankl arrives at the conclusion that "self-actualization is neither man's ultimate goal nor his primary intention." And even if it is a secondary intention, it presupposes that a man has been frustrated in his primary search for meanings to fulfill. Frankl likes to illustrate this point by the story about the boomerang that was given to him in Australia. He realized that the boomerang could be understood as a symbol of human existence: It is not the job of the boomerang to return, but to kill the prey. The boomerang returns to the hunter only if it missed the target. Similarly, Frankl adds, a man returns to himself and reflects upon himself and his self-actualization only if he missed his mission and is frustrated in his will to meaning.

Charlotte Bühler has said that people who speak of self-actualization really mean the fulfillment of their potentials. Seen in this manner, it would be a person's life task to actualize as many of his potentials as possible. But a person who blindly actualizes his potentials would feel neither self-actualization, nor self-realization, nor happiness. What he also must do is to evaluate his potentials and select them with a direction in mind. The "pursuit" of meaning implies choice of direction. Frankl quotes Socrates as having confessed to his potential to become a criminal. By actualizing this potential the great defender of law and justice would have become a common criminal. Frankl's point is readily supported by everyday experience: We know that there are many ways to be happy (to love someone or to dominate someone), many ways to actualize creativity (to create symphonies or atom bombs), many ways of self-realization (realization of what? One's artistic or one's practical self? One's cruel streak or one's compassion?). Thus, to the question "What am I able to do?" must be added the second question, "What am I called to do?"

Here, man's freedom of choice must be tempered by his responsibleness, and this is made more difficult by the fact that he rarely gets a second chance. As Frankl stresses in *Psychotherapy and Existentialism,* at every moment of a person's life several potentials present themselves, and it is not enough to actualize them; he must decide which to choose and thus make part of reality, and which to "condemn to nonbeing." Decisions are final: once actualized, what once was a potential can no longer be withdrawn and will have consequences which cannot be foreseen. Each life situation provides each person with the burdensome challenge to select the potentials he decides to make reality. And here, too, he has only his conscience to guide him, human and prone to error as it may be.

The Tensions of Healthy Man

This picture of man often is disturbing to students of logotherapy, especially those from the United States. "If that's the way we are," some have said, "no wonder we are in a state of anxiety. This constant demand to choose one potential out of many, to find the true meaning of a situation, to decide on the rank and order among seemingly colliding values, is bound to lead to mental anguish, particularly when the choices must be made under the pressure of time and on the basis of incomplete information."

Not so, logotherapy contends. It is true that the demand to make choices will lead to tensions, but these are healthy tensions expressing true human nature. They are the tensions which result from a person's stretching from what he is at present to what his vision tells him he can become in the future; the tensions between the "is" and the "ought." Gertrude Stein's verdict, "A rose is a rose is a rose," can be transferred to the animal kingdom but not to the human dimension. "A man is a man is a man" does not express the human condition. Man is not fully human if he is satisfied with the way he is rather than with what he ought to become.

In a similar vein, Frankl strongly opposes the current motiva-
tional theories which hold that man is primarily concerned
with maintaining his inner equilibrium and, to this end, with
reducing his tensions. He also denies that life's ultimate goal
is just to gratify one's drives and to satisfy one's needs and
instincts. Freud's pleasure principle, too, ultimately serves to
eliminate tensions; but to see man as continuously striving
for his inner equilibrium, Frankl warns, does not present the
complete picture — it holds no place for any true encounter
between man and the world. Such a view considers all of
man's actions only in the light of achieving equilibrium.
Parents raise their children to spare them conflicts; teachers
do not challenge their students but help them adjust; people
go to church (or to the analyst) to find peace of mind; they
form friendships to satisfy a need; they do good deeds to get
rid of a bad conscience. Everything is done not for the sake of
a cause or a person, but for the sake of inner equilibrium.
Thus, everything is devaluated to the level of a mere means to
an end — the end being to achieve a tensionless state.

So much for the homeostatic motivation as described by
Frankl; but he also points out that this striving for equilibrium is expressed by patients suffering from a sexual neurosis.
They speak of "masturbating on a woman." Such men use
their partner simply for the purpose of reducing sexual tension. This is the view of the neurotic. A healthy person will
not see others as only a means to an end. Such an attitude
would be an example of Martin Buber's I-it relationship,
where others are not seen as persons to be encountered but
only as things to be used.

Thus, in Frankl's view, man is not basically concerned
with pleasure and happiness to pursue, but rather with meaning to fulfill; he adds, however, that such meaning must be
outside and beyond himself. That meaning and values are
within man, and all he needs to do is to "realize his inner
self" is a popular but dangerous view. It is popular because
it saves man the effort to reach out for values — they are already in him. It is dangerous for exactly the same reason: by

saving man the effort to reach out, such a view breeds boredom and apathy, emptiness and meaninglessness. If people
don't reach out beyond themselves, but instead are content
with certain conditions within — such as self-actualization
and "peak experiences" — they will wind up with the existential vacuum or, as Frankl also calls it, an "abyss experience."

To pull a person out of this abyss, logotherapy prescribes
not the absence of tensions but, on the contrary, the challenge
of a sound amount of tension as contained in the tasks of daily
living. Mental well-being is seen as dependent on a sound
amount of tension that exists between man's being (what he
"is" now) and his meaning (what he "ought" to be, what he
is "meant" to be). That is why meaning must always be ahead
of being. "The meaning of meaning," Frankl stresses, "is to
set the pace of being."

The Pacemakers and the Peacemakers

He illustrates that point in *Psychiatry and Existentialism* with
a logotherapeutic interpretation of the Exodus story, when
God led the tribe of Israel through the wilderness into the
Promised Land. God, the Bible says, floated ahead of the
Israelites in the form of a cloud. God led them, was their
pacemaker. The wanderers in the wilderness would never
have been able to find their way into the Promised Land if
the cloud had not stayed ahead of them but had instead
settled among them: the cloud would have ceased to be a
leader and would have become a fog to confuse them.

In this manner, the transsubjective dimension is seen as
pacing man. Human history is the story of individuals reaching out beyond themselves. And it seems that one could go
even further and maintain that human progress is based on
the vision of a god ahead of man. An anthropology student at
the University of California developed the theory that primitive man never would have found the courage to domesticate
and ride a horse without the vision of swiftness he attributed
to his god of the hunt. Because the fastest animal he had ever

seen was the wild horse, he imagined his god on the back of
the fastest and wildest horse. Only after he had become
familiar with the idea of such an image, could he conceive the
thought of seeing himself on horseback. And once man conceives a goal, he finds the courage to reach for it. God is
always the example, the ultimate force that coaxes man along
to deeds that first were only daring dreams. Man forever
reaches for God's exclusive fire and for the fruit of His exclusive tree. Man always endowed his god with the qualities
man himself longed for: to fly through the air, to destroy his
enemies, to conquer disease and death. Thus, he pictured his
god as winged, powerful, eternal. And man, following the
Eternal Pacemaker, managed to make many of his former
dreams come true: man flies faster than Mercury and is ap-
proaching the destructive power of Jahweh; he has conquered
many diseases and is beginning to talk about old age as if one
day it, too, may be conquerable. Yet, some qualities of the
Pacemaker remain unreached, perhaps unreachable: to know
truth, to be just and wise, to know good from evil, to know
life's meaning.

God's quality of being a Pacemaker has itself become a
goal of man. Religious leaders, poets, explorers, philosophers,
teachers, parents — they all have wanted to be, and often were,
pacemakers. Recently, however, a generation of men has
grown up that is pursuing a different goal. Not that of pacemakers, but "peacemakers," although not in the sense the
Bible uses the word when speaking of the "blessed peacemakers" who shall be called "the children of God." Frankl,
in introducing the distinction between pacemakers and peacemakers in *Psychiatry and Existentialism,* says that the pacemakers confront man with challenges; the peacemakers stress
internal peace of mind and are trying to spare him confrontations. According to this view, Moses was a pacemaker: he
never attempted to make it easy on his people; he brought the
Ten Commandments to the Israelites, and not only confronted them with high ideals, but pointed out to them how
far short they fell.

By contrast, peacemakers — as Frankl portrays them — take the opposite approach. Concerned with man's "inner equilibrium," they do not confront him with ideals, but with facts. They do not make him stretch his vista, but assure him that everything is fine the way it is. They are the ones who try to persuade their fellow man that meanings are inside him and that he need not bother reaching out; that adjustment, not reaching, is the goal in life. The peacemakers of the present think in terms not of ideals but norms; they do not trust in hopes and dreams but in statistics and opinion polls. They talk about the "average" person instead of the unique individual, but the average person can find no meaning because there is no average meaning. The peacemakers supply the facts that are comforting to the majority: "Why bother with ideals? Why be different from the average? If most husbands cheat on their wives, why should I be faithful? If most people tell lies, why should I be truthful?" The goal of the peacemakers is to make people, not good or wise or just, but "normal." One American student of logotherapy has commented upon the irony of the language: seen from this point of view, most of the present-day warmakers must be classified as "peacemakers" — they do not think of the effect of war on human beings and values; they think in terms of logistics, efficiency of destruction, cost-per-enemy-killed, and in an effort to "adjust to the facts of life" they accept the standards of the enemy they are fighting.

The United States, at the time of its founding, was a great pacemaker for the entire Western world. The new country was an example in democracy, individualism, freedom, and personal responsibility. The resulting upsurge of optimism and purposefulness lasted more than a century. Now, however, there is evidence that the United States has become a peacemaker. The ideals of democracy have been frozen into a worship of the *status quo*. The Declaration of Independence is a revered document, no longer a living example. Individual freedom has become entangled in the complexities of modern government in a heavily populated country. The responsibility of decision making has been transferred from the individual to the anonymity of committees, organizations, and government agencies. Our shift, as a country, from a pacemaker (concerned with values) to a peacemaker (concerned with facts) may well account for the widespread feeling of apathy and meaninglessness. Americans sense the loss of values and ideals that were held high by their forefathers who were the pacemakers of liberation and revolution in the Western world. In those days, the United States was a revolutionary country in a conservative world. Today it is a conservative country in a revolutionary world. But a *status-quo* society has no challenge, only equilibrium. Its goals are pleasure and power, not ideals and meanings, although the ideals and meanings of earlier times are enshrined and worshiped. In reality, though, those early Puritan traits of independence, individual responsibleness, inventiveness, bootstrap ambition, and honesty are giving way to a new set of goals among which are bigness, material well-being, *status quo,* social security, a well-balanced personality, and a good image.

There is hopeful evidence, however, that wide segments of the population in the United States have a longing for their country to become a pacemaker again. This longing found expression during the Kennedy administration which openly challenged the American people to respond to individual tasks. On his American visits during that period, Frankl delighted in buying souvenirs that featured Kennedy's phrase, "Ask not what your country will do for you; ask what you can do for your country." It is extremely unlikely that President Kennedy ever came across Frankl's first American book, *The Doctor and the Soul,* but there a similar thought had been phrased as, "Man should not ask what he may expect from life, but should rather understand that life expects something from him." That Kennedy's appeal fell on fertile ground became obvious by the response of America's youth to the Peace Corps. Americans want their country to become a pacemaker again, and not merely remain the image of a former pacemaker, and that desire spans the entire political spectrum from the New Left to the conservative Right. The conscience of the Left is concerned with the freedom of the individual against enforced loyalty oaths and school prayers and even the draft; with the responsibleness of the white man toward the black; with the democratic idea to let people everywhere choose their own government even if it means revolution. The Right, although rejecting most of the goals of the Left, also reaches for the ideals of the pacemaker. They call for a return to individualism, personal responsibility, freedom from government interference, and they talk about the American people's unrest and despair as a consequence of regimentation. Senator Goldwater, who, as a Presidential candidate in 1964, was the spokesman of this mood, declared in his acceptance speech that he perceived in this country "a virtual despair among the many who look beyond material success to the inner meaning of their lives." In speech after speech he reiterated, in Calvinistic terms, the same virtues of which Frankl speaks in logotherapeutic terms: values, ideals, personal responsibility, and reliance on one's own conscience — in Goldwater's case, the "Conscience of a Conservative."

Meaning in the Affluent Society

Also during the 1964 Presidential election campaign, another spokesman of conservatism, the *Wall Street Journal*, posed the question why such manifestations of vague uneasiness should appear in the midst of general affluence.

Trying to answer that question from a logotherapeutic point of view, one is tempted to say that still another of mankind's most persistent "pursuits," namely that of Utopia — the ultimate in affluence and tensionlessness — also is a mirage. Frankl claims that a complete satisfaction of man's needs and drives would not lead to happiness but, on the contrary, to a frustrating inner void, a desperate feeling of emptiness. A look at history seems to bear this out. The Pilgrims, facing a strange and hostile continent, did not feel an existential vacuum; they had a task to fulfill. Societies under stress produced people who found meaning in overcoming their difficulties — from the Israelites wandering in the wilderness to the French under German occupation in World War II. Boredom and emptiness became prevalent in times of plenty and material security — among the freemen of the Roman Empire at the peak of its power, among the aristocrats at the court of Louis XVI, and now among the prosperous of affluent America. The social critic Lewis Mumford put it in strong words: "The expanding American economy for all its suffocating abundance of machine-made goods and gadgets has resulted in a dismally contracted life, lived for the most part confined to a car or a television set; a life so empty of vivid firsthand experiences that it might as well be lived in a space capsule, traveling from nowhere to nowhere at supersonic speeds."[2] Twenty years ago, the Viennese logotherapist Paul Polak had warned against the belief that neuroses would disappear when man had solved his economic problems. Polak predicted that only then would the existential questions rise to the top of man's conscience.

This, apparently, is happening in the affluent societies in the West. Some of the most ancient tensions of mankind — those caused by the struggle to find food and shelter, and protection against the hostilities of nature — have been drastically reduced; others are adjusted away, pampered away, and tranquilized away. Under the influence of the peacemakers, man goes to great lengths to avoid tension. Yet, people do not become happier. The strange thing is, observes Frankl, that if they are spared tensions they create them, either in a healthy or an unhealthy way. The most popular way to create healthy tensions, he thinks, is sports: it is the function of sports, at least of the more active types, to allow people to live out the need for tension by imposing demands upon themselves. This is a truly human activity. No other animal puts up hurdles in order to jump over them, or climbs rocks simply to overcome the difficulty. But tensions may be built up in many unhealthy ways, too. As Frankl points out, young people, particularly if they are not confronted sufficiently with tasks, find dangerous areas in which to look for tension. They defy authority, provoke the police, play hooky from school, commit senseless crimes, and risk their lives without good reason by "playing chicken" or arranging "Brazilian duels." But the existential vacuum of youth need not be filled with destructive contents, as demonstrated in Oslo, Norway, where youthful hooligans who had satisfied their desire for tension by slashing tires and streetcar seats, formed a patrol to prevent such activities of competing gangs. To their own surprise, they found it just as "exciting" to be on the side of the law as to fight it.

A Return to Ideals

On his visits to the United States Frankl is understandably hesitant to criticize his host country, but he has, on occasions, commented on the Americans' great hankering for the tensionless society and, more specifically, on Freud's unintentional influence in this respect. In an article published (and commented on by Abraham Maslow) in the *Journal of Humanistic Psychology* in 1966, Frankl points out that Freud's era was one of tension, especially tension aroused by the widespread repression of sex. This tension, thanks to Freud, has been released, and this brought great relief to the Anglo-Saxon countries which had long been suffering from the restrictions of a Puritan heritage. In a mass reaction against the unrealistic overdemand of "virtues" made by Puritanism, Americans have gone on a rampage of "underdemand." They have become afraid of demanding too much of their young, and a system of education developed which carefully refrained from challenging students with "Puritan" concepts such as ideals and values. Frankl calls this "a case of dumping the baby out with the bath water." Not only Puritan ideals, but *all* ideals were dismissed as something outdated. It was considered "twentieth century" to be factual and materialistic. But he sees a return to the challenge of ideals. He quotes

Louis J. West, the head of the Department of Behavioral Sciences at the Oklahoma School of Medicine, who said, "Our youth can afford idealism because they are the first generation of the affluent society. But they cannot afford materialism, dialectic or capitalistic, because they are also the first generation which truly may see the end of the world. Our young men and women are educated enough to know that only an ideal of human brotherhood can save the world and them."[3] This is commitment, not to the tasks of yesterday but to those of tomorrow. Frankl also quotes — not only depth psychologists but what he facetiously calls a "height" psychologist — the first American astronaut, John H. Glenn, who said, "Ideals are the very stuff of survival."[4] Ideals, commitments, tasks are becoming respectable again, not only in speeches and sermons, but in action.

Reducing meanings and values to psychologically and sociologically determined projections of one's inner makeup could not erode the natural idealism of the young American nation. American youth commits itself to many causes — the Peace Corps, the war on poverty, civil rights, freedom of speech, peace. Ministers leave their pulpits to march. Scientists leave their laboratory facts and actively support political candidates. Students leave their classrooms to demonstrate. Is that unhealthy? Yes, if it is done to run away from one's existential vacuum, but not if it is done to give one's life a worthy content. The chief of the psychiatric clinic of the student hospital at the University of California, Berkeley, at the time of the student free-speech demonstrations disclosed that admission to the clinic had dropped to almost zero, but that the incidence of neuroses increased again as soon as the demonstrations were over. Here is support for the thesis that mental health depended on having a meaning to fulfill, an ideal to reach toward.

The times are full of challenges. Even in an affluent society, man need not look very far for tasks to fulfill. All he needs to do is to widen his horizon beyond his own self, beyond his immediate family, friends, beyond his in-groups, and even beyond his nation, and he will see that while he lives in affluence, many others live in poverty and need his help. In an address before the Congress for Health and Education in Stockholm, Sweden, Frankl commented: "Thousands of years ago the Jewish tribe developed the awareness of monotheism, the idea of one God. Perhaps the time has come to take a second giant step and develop the awareness of what I would like to call 'monanthropism,' the idea of one mankind; the awareness that we are all members of one humanity regardless of color, religion, and political beliefs. Once we are aware of this, no one will look for tasks in vain, and life will once again have meaning."

CHAPTER VII

Our Crumbling Traditions

Things most taken for granted need most to be doubted. . . .
Don't let yourself be hypnotized by traditional solutions.

PIET HEIN

LOGOTHERAPY MAINTAINS that today's widespread feeling of emptiness is the result of a double loss that man has suffered: the loss of both his instincts and his traditions.

Animals get direction for their lives and behavior through their instincts. Man was deprived of his basic animal instincts long before the beginning of history — "his instinctual security, like paradise, is closed to him forever," Frankl says. Man does not have the salmon's drive to the mountain spring of his origins, nor the bear's impulse toward the warm cave when winter is threatening. Man must find the direction of his life through his capacity to reach out for the meanings of his existence. But he must also rely on values handed down from generation to generation, by tradition, through such human institutions as the family, church, school, and state.

Periods of Rapid Change

In normal times, tradition will guide man in his conduct. However, there come periods when man's trust in his traditions and institutions breaks down. He is left without directions, and anxiety results. Paul Tillich, in his book *The Courage to Be,* lists three sources of anxiety: death (the fear of nothingness); guilt (the awareness of having violated a moral law); and meaninglessness (the raising of questions for which no answer can be found). Tillich points out that at the end of antiquity man's anxiety was concerned with fear of death, and religions such as Christianity emerged, which were preoccupied with immortality and resurrection. At the end of the Middle Ages man was concerned with his guilt, and with moral anxieties, for which the Reformation offered a way to forgiveness and atonement. Now man has reached the end of another period which, for lack of a better name, is called modern times (although he has passed through "modern times" and entered a new, as yet unnamed, era), and this period is dominated by the anxiety caused by a feeling of meaninglessness. Conceivably, man's present concern with the meaning of life will give birth to a new movement, possibly based on existentialism — theological, atheistic, psychological, or some other form. With guidance by the instincts lost, and traditions in a state of disrepute, it is quite possible that man will have to acquire the direction of his life existentially.

At the end of each of the three periods — antiquity, the Middle Ages, and modern times — long-accepted values were questioned, established institutions lost their power, and traditions were mistrusted. Possibly, this breakdown is more virulent today than in the previous transition periods. It is not the first time that man's concepts of his deity have undergone changes, that his trust in established civil and church authorities has been shaken, that his relationships within his society and family have shifted. In his relentless search for truth man has climbed many summits that provided vistas different from those to which he was accustomed. But now the thrusts of science are coming so fast that man has no tradition to guide him in dealing with his new knowledge. For the first time the differences between the old and the new are so enormous that mere changes in quantity amount also to changes in quality. For instance, man can look back on a long string of weapons, each one always deadlier than the one preceding. Man has faced destruction before — of his person, his family, his tribe — but never the destruction of his planet. The H-bomb is more than a new weapon — it is a new way of life and death, forcing man to take a new look at such ancient concepts as war and peace, courage, honor, loyalty, and patriotism. Population increase, the ambition of every country from the times of the Bible up to World War II, has become a threat, requiring man to reexamine not only the values of his life but also those of unborn life. Space travel is not merely another means of transportation in the development from the wheel to rocketry, it literally opens up the universe, expanding man's view of himself, life, and divinity, as the universe itself expands before his telescopic observations. Man has come to realize that he is in search, not in possession, of truth. The search for truth has led him from ignorance and superstition to the position of a biochemical imitator of God, a potential genetic co-creator, and at the same time the search has opened up an even vaster abyss of human ignorance. It has led him from an era of smug certainty to one of doubt that extends to all fields of knowledge. Walter Lippmann, writer and columnist, was one of the first to become aware of the impending fundamental changes when he wrote, as early as 1914, in *Drift and Mastery:* "No mariner ever enters upon a more uncharted sea than does the average human being born in the twentieth century. Our ancestors thought they knew their way from birth to eternity; we are puzzled about the day after tomorrow." Today, one generation after these words were written, every value and tradition is under attack from some quarter. Yet, as Lippmann also pointed out, the overthrow of tradition and ancient laws, however outdated, will not bring a meaningful life, just as democracy does not automatically establish itself when a king is overthrown, or men become cooperative when the propertied class is defeated.

A Breakdown of Values

Ever since man started on his voyage of discovery, he has developed values which he has slowly modified and eventually discarded. This process has been so slow that one generation did not notice the breakdown of values. Today the breakdown is spreading so fast that it has opened the greatest value

gap between generations in history, and — again quoting
Lippmann — has spread to affect many traditional cornerstones. Among those that have crumbled within our lifetime
are the sanctity of property, hereditary caste, the dogma of
sin, blind obedience to authority, and even the value of tradition itself. An increasing number of people will not accept
the mere age of an institution as a reason for believing in it.
Many of today's youngsters do not trust anyone over thirty;
children do not trust their parents; citizens, their government; students, their professors; churchgoers, and even theologians, the religious dogmas. No citadel of tradition has
remained intact.

When Frankl visited Japan, he spoke to his audiences
about their high level of culture, their old traditions, and the
extremely rapid change in their cultural patterns — their
abolishing of traditions within twenty years after having
followed them for two thousand. In a question period a
young girl stood up and asked, "How can we find meaning in
this age of vanishing traditions and values?" The question
made him aware that he ought to stress the changing role of
education — not only that in school and home, but also the
educational functions of all civil and religious authorities.

So he told his Japanese audiences that, for thousands of
years, it had been the task of education to pass on values from
generation to generation. But in our time of changing values
and fading tradition, the particular mission of education is
shifting. It is to help people refine their individual conscience because the less a person can rely on the guidance of
traditional values, the more he must rely on his own capacity
to find the unique meanings in each situation of his life.
Universal values can break down but not the unique meanings of his personal life.

The sudden breakdown of values was the experience of the
Austrian Jews when Hitler annexed that country. On March
11, 1938, the Jews in Vienna saw the sudden collapse of the
country they had loved, the government they had trusted, the
society they had grown up in, the family that had protected

them, the laws that had guaranteed their safety. Honesty turned out not to be the best policy, and it became necessary to lie in order to survive. Father was not always right, and often paid with his life for following his own advice to wait quietly until things calmed down. The government did the murdering and stealing which traditionally it had prohibited by law. The synagogues were burned down, and the churches, at best, were silent. The Cardinal of Vienna issued a proclamation supporting the godless regime. The Austrian Jew of 1938 found himself in a moral no-man's land, with no signposts. What were the highest values? Survival? Courage? Honor? Cunning? Material advantages? He found no ends to strive for, only means, and the means ran wild. And then it dawned on him that in this wilderness he had nowhere to turn, that he was on his own.

The Refugee as a Guinea Pig

This was the traumatic experience of the refugee in 1938. But meanwhile, throughout the next thirty years, the breakdown of traditional values has been spreading to the "settled" people in an affluent society. One might think of the refugees of the Thirties as the guinea pigs for a gruesome experiment affecting everyone in the Sixties: the experiment to find out how to survive and retain one's sense of meaning in the face of eroding values, fading traditions, and vanishing institutions; how to live in a world that denies man the guidance of values and, at the same time, cuts him off from the personal source of meaning, his conscience. One danger of his being cut off from his conscience lies in his continuing "reification," the treatment of man as if he were a thing, because a thing has no conscience. It was Hitler's devilish scheme that he not only treated his victims as things but that he also succeeded, by pressure and propaganda, in convincing many, but never all, of his victims that they were things and had no recourse to their conscience.

In his essay, "Say Yes to Life in Spite of Everything,"

Frankl describes life in the concentration camp as the supreme degradation of the worth of man. Imagine, he says, the state squeezing the last few drops of life out of human beings it has already condemned to death, forcing work out of them rather than killing them outright or feeding them without getting some use from them. "How often were we told in the concentration camps that we were not worth the soup fed to us — this soup which was our only warm meal and which we were to earn by digging ditches. We, the worthless ones, had to receive this unearned gift in proper gratitude: we had to take off our cap when we stood in line for it. Our life was no longer worth a bowl of soup, our death not worth a bullet — only a whiff of gas." This soup became no more than the oil necessary to keep a piece of machinery going a while longer. Man was a thing to be used as long as he was usable, to be discarded as efficiently and cheaply as possible when he was worn out. The same philosophy led to the mass killings in mental institutions: the patient was considered a faulty piece of equipment and therefore useless.

The Hitler refugee in the Thirties, trying to find a safe spot to survive, was probably the closest to being a thing of any that existed in human form outside the concentration camp. But the horrible aspect of it was (and this aspect was spared the inmate of the concentration camp who still could retain the illusion that his situation was a horrible exception) that Hitler was able to make the world join him in considering the Jew as a surplus commodity. Nothing illustrates this point more clearly than the Evian Conference at which Hitler offered the world 40,000 Jews for sale, at $25,000 apiece, and some thirty nations rejected the offer. Individual nations made offers of their own, not based on what the refugees were (human beings) but on what they had (money, skills, knowledge). Bolivia allowed a trickle of human merchandise across its borders if the immigrants were young and qualified farmers or investors with at least 1,000 pounds sterling; Haiti restricted immigration to those possessing $5,000; Kenya narrowed its imports to those with 500 pounds; Paraguay to those with 1,500 gold dollars and the knowledge necessary for establishing new industries. Those who did not have what the market demanded, found themselves dumped, often literally, into the ocean (on ramshackle boats that were not allowed to land anywhere) or burned (in concentration camps, like surplus Brazilian coffee).

If Man Is a Thing . . .

In consequence, six million humans perished, a monstrous toll in any kind of experiment. But one might somehow accept this loss (even if among those vanished were one's parents, spouse, or friends) if one could see it as a sacrifice with some meaning behind it. Even the meaning of a warning: This is what happens when humans are treated as figures on transportation lists, as bookkeeping problems, as problems in efficient disposal. One can accept such mass misery — barely — as a warning that "it can happen here," in civilized countries, if man — for whatever reasons — is considered a thing. But the warning is not being heard. What Hitler did to his victims, man now does to himself, proudly and in the name of progress. For man is well on his way to regarding himself as a mere object if political parties become bureaucracies in which the voter is merely a statistic in a poll, if economists consider the human being as a consumer to be brainwashed by advertisements, if management sees in him a tool to be replaced by more efficient machinery, labor uses him as a pawn in a bargaining process, the universities handle him as an IBM card and process him toward acquiring the skills the market demands. The reification of man may happen, not in the misery of death camps, but in the namelessness of urban renewal that is building spiritual slums; in the graphs and charts in which human tragedy is presented: the unemployed, the school dropouts, the delinquents, the crime casualties, the traffic accidents; in modern warfare in which potential casualties are calculated, not in terms of six million victims but of sixty million, where killing is not performed by personal confrontation with the enemy but by the push-button. In the military world of today, personal bravery is less important than technical knowledge and psychological adapt-ability to teamwork and crowded living. The commanding officer is becoming the manager of a complex administration, dealing not with human beings but with objects. At the same time, civilian production is becoming increasingly uniform, demanding greater conformity, the obeying of orders (al-though persuasion takes the place of blind command, brief-ings replace orders); and teamwork and committees are considered superior to individual decisions. Even the military hero and the political leader, considered by many the greatest individuals in the past, tend to become mere images that can be manipulated like electrical forces.

Once man becomes a thing he has no tradition, only ob-solescence; or, as Frankl observes, man then has no "values," only "uses." But for such a "thing" reality can no longer be meaningful. Paul Tillich, in *Theology of Culture*, sees con-temporary man as "a cog within a universal machine to which he must adapt himself in order not to be smashed by it. But this adaptation makes him a means for ends which are means themselves, and in which an ultimate end is lacking. Out of this predicament of man in the industrial society, the experi-ences of emptiness and meaninglessness, of dehumanization and estrangement, have resulted." Because man, as a thing among things, no longer can encounter reality as meaning-ful, Tillich says, he may withdraw to a limited section of reality, defend it against the intrusion of the world, and thus become a neurotic; or he may lose contact with reality al-together, and become a psychotic. Such withdrawal, Tillich concludes, results in the repression of the question of mean-ing.

When discussing man's self-made reification, Frankl some-times speaks of the "propaganda of nonmeaning" to which man has been exposed to such an extent that he becomes apologetic when talking about meanings and values. In this connection he also likes to credit Immanuel Kant, who, even before the onset of the industrial revolution, had been aware of this trend toward reification. Kant maintained that everything had its value but that man had his worth, and that he must never be regarded as a means to an end. Since the time of Kant, man has gone through the industrial era and has entered the era of automation which makes him a means for producing goods. Man has entered the era of mass advertisement which makes him a means for selling products. He has entered the era of political cynicism which makes him a means for maneuvering votes. The great numbers in population make it difficult to pay attention to individuals, and lead to regimentation in the name of orderliness; and regimentation, again, tends to make man a means for the efficient functioning of things.

Groping for a Cure

Having diagnosed the ills of our times, Frankl tries to point the direction toward a cure. His cure — the return to the resources of one's personal conscience — is neither unique nor new; but what is novel is his challenge that education, in the broadest sense, must lead man back to the resources of his conscience and help him refine his conscience. These thoughts are not yet widespread in his writings. They are found in recent seminar lectures and in his latest journal articles, such as "Self-Transcendence as a Human Phenomenon" in the Fall 1966 issue of the *Journal of Humanistic Psychology,* and "What Is Meant by Meaning?" in the Winter 1966 issue of the *Journal of Existentialism.*

In these seminars and articles he sees "conscience as the intuitive capacity to perceive the unique meaning *gestalt* of the unique life situation," but also recognizes that in the very young, meaning must be channeled through the experiences of older people:

> You cannot expect a very small child to have a fully developed conscience, nor does he any longer possess the bulk of instincts of the animals. Thus he must be guided by ex-

periences which previous generations found useful and meaningful — both on the individual and on the social level. A
person's early education must take the form of values handed
down from the elders. But as the child grows up, he becomes
more and more able to take a stand that is independent of traditions, and he may even oppose traditions. For this man has
to pay. The emergence of what I call noögenic neuroses is
due to the conflict between man's true conscience and his
mere superego — that superego which is channeling traditions and values held dear by his societal environment.

The Danger of Mummification

It has been said that it is the function of tradition to trans-
mute knowledge into wisdom and pass it on to the individuals
who cannot possibly accumulate the wisdom of the ages by
their own experiences. It is generally accepted that the young
person growing up needs guidance, sometimes to the point of
demand for blind obedience. Responsible parents will insist
that their small child obey certain rules with no questions
asked: the child cannot afford to learn by trial and error the
danger of walking into a fire or crossing a street against the
traffic. For the same reason primitive societies develop complex rituals, and sophisticated societies give their authorities
the right to make and enforce laws; not every generation has
the time and opportunity to find out by itself what is
true and false, right and wrong, good and bad, what is desirable and what must be avoided. To have the guidance of
childhood rules, rituals, religiously approved values, and
civil laws gives people security and direction. For this reason,
tradition, which passes on these rules and values, must not be
blindly disregarded. It contains the accumulated wisdom of
the ages; by discarding tradition indiscriminately, man is in
danger of throwing out not only its outdated and objection-
able trimmings but also the time-tested truths at its core.
Besides, tradition probably cannot be discarded altogether because dependence on outer authority is so deep in man's bones
that it has become a tradition itself.

Tradition is a blessing that comes from the past, but also a curse that threatens the future. Blind acceptance of tradition can be as dangerous as blind rejection because it mummifies values in a continually changing world. Today's facts are tomorrow's absurdity, and today's dream is tomorrow's reality. As a person matures, he checks his traditional values against his life's experiences, and they won't always fit. The same goes for maturing societies. Knowledge increases, and the wisdom based on this evolving knowledge must occasionally be brought up to date. Even encyclopedias become outdated and have to be revised. Most of the change is so gradual it is hardly noticed. Yet, the gradual changes accumulate over centuries until the original laws and customs would not be recognized even by their founders. The story is told in the Jewish Talmud (Menahot, 29 b) how Moses came down to earth and visited the school of the great scholar Rabbi Akiba who taught in the first century. Moses sat down in the last row and listened. But he did not understand what the sage was teaching until Akiba closed his lecture with the words, "This is the law that Moses received on Sinai."

The danger comes from those who insist that they have found the truth once and for all. While the values passed on by tradition may open the doors to age-old wisdom, they may also imprison if they are not constantly checked against the reality of growing knowledge. Nothing, neither a man nor a value, can be preserved by being locked up. A man will not stop his aging process in prison, and morals cannot be stopped from becoming outdated simply because they are locked up in rules, laws, rituals, or holy books. Without constant change the most glorious tradition becomes a dead weight. Arturo Toscanini is said to have shouted to the musicians at rehearsals, "Routine — the death of music!" It is also the death of ethics, wisdom, and truth. Here is the basis for logotherapy's appeal to man, stressing the uniqueness of meaning over the universality of values.

Routinely and blindly accepted values are dangerous even in times of normal human development. They may prove catastrophic in times of rapid changes. Occasionally human knowledge comes in such rapid bursts that tradition has no chance to absorb all the newly found truths. In such situations, man — checking his traditional values against the experiences of a vastly changed world — finds tradition no reliable guide. He feels insecure, confused; and he cannot find meanings by following outdated values. This may have happened in Biblical times, and perhaps this is what the story of the Tower of Babel is trying to convey: that man attempted to build his tower of knowledge too high and too fast, and too close to the secrets of God, and the result was confusion. In historical times, periods of confusion occurred sporadically, for instance in ancient Greece in the fifth pre-Christian century when scientific discoveries revolutionized man's picture of his world, his gods, and himself; again at the end of the medieval period when a torrent of inventions and explorations radically changed man's outlook on the world as he knew it. And it is happening today. We are living through an era of unprecedented expansion of human knowledge.

The Source of Unique Meanings

When traditions and established institutions are no longer trusted and universal values are breaking down, each individual is thrown back on his own resources of painstakingly searching for the unique meanings of his life situation. For, according to logotherapist beliefs, the unique meanings of man's life situations remain even if universal values should become discredited.

However, Frankl maintained that values can never disappear completely. Part of them can be cast off, others can change, but some universal values will always remain because no individual lives on an island: "He shares typical life situations with others." From this common ground universal values keep emerging. Even in times when traditional values become discredited and most people float in a sea of apparent meaninglessness, he was certain that some individuals would have a conscience alert enough to discover the meaning of the changed situation. "And the meanings of today become the values of tomorrow."

That might have happened in Greece at the time of Socrates, in Palestine at the time of Jesus, in India at the time of Buddha. "Traditions fell apart," Frankl speculated, "and a feeling of emptiness developed. But then the founders of religions stood up and not only discovered new meanings of their own, but also set up new ideals to transmit. It is the 'in-between' periods that bring on the existential vacuum."

The In-Between Periods

The prospect that the present in-between period may be one of those turbulent intervals of transition, which can be overcome only by the fresh insights of men with refined conscience, has prompted speculation about the emergence of new "prophets" who will show the way. The names of Gandhi, Schweitzer, Buber, and others have been mentioned. Perhaps the new prophet is wandering the earth, unknown, as Jesus was unknown during the first thirty years of his life; perhaps he has not even been born yet. Possibly the new message will come not through one Messiah but through a multitude. This was the hope of Lewis Mumford who, fifteen years ago, in his *Conduct of Life,* suggested that "mankind's security and salvation" might be achieved "if one person in ten were fully awakened, fully capable of exercising his higher centers of intelligence and morality." Mumford felt that, especially in a democracy, man cannot shift the burden, as he has done in the past, to an Emperor, a Messiah, a dictator, or a single Godlike man, but that the task of the individual Messiah of the past now devolves equally upon all men, and that this task also carries the burden of sacrifice. There are indications that the young generation of today is ready to shoulder the burden and the sacrifice of the Messiah. Students, civil rights workers, and other youthful demonstrators let themselves be ridiculed, arrested, and shot at, and are risking social and economic ostracism for causes they think worth supporting. And the church, normally the staunchest upholder of the *status quo,* to some extent at least, supports the rebels through its ministers, priests, and rabbis who not only preach, but also participate in demonstrations. In a meeting of churchmen, commemorating ministers martyred in the civil-rights movement, discussion turned to the possibility that the prophets of today may not necessarily be, as in bygone days, solitary old men, but groups of the young. The ministers admitted that many of the protesting youngsters, probably the majority, were neither reformers nor prophets but rather conformists to their own subculture of protesters. Some of them, however, at least displayed the characteristics of reformers (protesting against what they believe to be wrong) and others had true prophetic qualities (advocating what they believe to be right). The prophetic group, although a minority, is showing genuine moral concern for the issues of the present. They are doing what the prophets of old did — pointing the way to new values, and taking the same burdens: ridicule, arrest, death. It may just be possible that their views will prevail, and show mankind the direction of a new morality. The new morality must come, as it always has, from individuals, and must concern itself not so much with material well-being, as with ethics. *Time* magazine, on January 6, 1967, reported a short dialogue between two of those young prophets who gave up two years of their affluent lives to follow the call of their conscience. Said Laurance Rockefeller, Jr., 22, great-grandson of John D., working as a $22.50-a-week Vista volunteer in Harlem, New York: "Beyond affluence, what?" Answered co-Vista-worker Tweed Roosevelt, 24, great-grandson of Teddy: "Individualism."

The Role of Education

According to the concepts of logotherapy, a new morality cannot develop from a vacuum; it must be built up from fresh insights of individuals whose consciences are refined enough to see the unique meanings through the thicket of universal, but often outdated, values. Frankl feels that education can play a major part in guiding the young toward finding meaning. "It will become the assigned task of education," he stated, "to refer man to his conscience and help him refine it. With the aid of a well-educated, trained, and refined conscience, we shall always be able to see meanings — the unique meanings inherent in the unique situations of our life."

This seemingly unorthodox goal of education is actually at least 2,500 years old. It is the extension of Plato's concept that the purpose of education is the enlightenment of the ruler so that he might be the philosopher-king, the best informed, the most sensitive to the needs of the day, the man with the most responsive conscience. In a democracy, where everyone is the ruler, everyone needs to become so informed, sensitive, and responsive.

Man, even in the most advanced democracies of the twentieth century, is barely at the edge of such a concept. But Frankl would like to see education accept the task of challenging the students to find new values, and to discover the rank and order of existing values — not the value hierarchy as it has been inherited from the older generation, but as the students themselves feel, in their conscience, it ought to exist today. Frankl discussed the subject of "Value Dimensions in Teaching" in his video tape interview with Huston Smith, professor of philosophy at MIT, and admitted that education was limited in teaching values "because values cannot be taught, they must be lived; nor can meanings be given by the teacher. What a teacher may give his students is not a meaning but an example: the example of his personal dedication and devotion to the great cause of science, truth, and research." The teacher must challenge the students to find meanings by setting the example of his own commitment. In addition, Frankl added, the teacher should take heed not to undermine the basic meaning orientation of the youngsters by presenting them with a relativistic and subjectivistic philosophy of life. And he stressed again the importance of not counteracting the original enthusiasm and idealism of youth, their deep concern with values and ideals, by teaching them, for example, that values are "nothing but defense mechanisms and reaction formations." This view is supported by some university teachers, such as Nevitt Sanford of Stanford's psychology department who wrote in the *American Journal of Psychiatry* that a teacher cannot be effective unless he is prepared to deal with these issues (values and ideals) and does not regard every moral stand that a student takes as some expression of his resistance. A teacher has "to be able to carry on the discourse with students in strictly ethical terms."[1]

Students are often taught that human existence can be explained only in terms of either the "machine model" or the "rat model" (to use a sarcastic phrase from Gordon W. Allport, a well-known critic of such models). Such a mechanistic kind of teaching is likely to undermine the students' belief in their freedom to make decisions. To what extent even high school students are being indoctrinated by such a deterministic approach is apparent in the experience of college advisors. They find that many entering freshmen, after being counseled, are happily surprised to hear that they still can change — that even at the ripe age of eighteen they may still alter the direction of their lives.

The role of education in overcoming the present transition period between the eras of obsolete traditions and newly emerging values is of concern to writers and educators both East and West. Krishnamurti maintains that only the man who does not follow tradition can discover what is true; that a man cannot leave the shelter of tradition and inquire, observe, learn, and be deeply aware, if he is afraid; and that the function of education is to eradicate this fear that destroys human thought, human relationship, and love. In the West the role of education is seen by an elite group of educators (whose spokesman is Robert Hutchins, former Chancellor of the University of Chicago) as a beacon rather than as a mirror of society — a restatement of Frankl's demand that education make the young a generation of "pacemakers" reaching out for new goals, rather than "peacemakers" adjusting to the old. Hutchins criticizes education's "service-station approach" which caters to the wishes of society, with all its mistaken goals, and treats society as a customer who is always right. The student is not educated, but trained to do what society wants and pays for. In a recent convocation of the Center for the Study of Democratic Institutions, of which he is now president, Hutchins spoke of American education as a system whereby young people are fitted into the existing environment, and which prepares them to adjust to the requirements of society and the job market, and trains them to accept values rather than challenge values. "Students," Hutchins concluded on a note of optimism, "are looking for tasks and challenges; they do not want to fit into a society like automatons."[2]

At the same convocation, Clarence Faust, President of the Fund for the Advancement of Education, regretted that the universities confirm currently accepted opinions, ideologies, even prejudices of the day, and submit to loyalty oaths and legislative watchdog committees. Walter Lippmann called on the universities to accept their task to fill the spiritual and intellectual vacuum and provide guidance for their students in an age in which man has been "deprived of the guidance and support of traditional and customary authority." Rosemary Park, President of Barnard College, challenged college administrators to become "a kind of Socrates . . . asking the hurrying faculty what they mean by truth, justice, decency, even academic freedom. And we must ask the students . . . what they mean by integrity and how they recognize it, and, most important of all, what they think is going on." This, Miss Park felt, "will begin the creation of a moral core, as Socrates' questions sought to clarify the will of Athens."[3]

New Values in Education

Nevitt Sanford pointed out that education must do more than emphasize values. Everyone is in favor of values — but which values? Education stresses excellence, for instance, but excellence in what? As a scientist or as a person? Is it enough for a university to train specialists in their fields, scientists who will make brilliant discoveries, without considering how they will be used? The universities can produce great physicists, chemists, and engineers, but unless they also produce conscientious human beings who care about their fellowmen, the new knowledge will be misused. Even the most brilliant physician is not always the greatest humanitarian, and the excellent mechanic may be wanting in excellence as a person. It is significant that Medicare was not suggested by physicians, nor car safety laws by mechanics; on the contrary, these laws were widely opposed by the specialists. Good teaching, Sanford feels, must include lessons for students on how to make individual decisions, and this capacity must be sharpened on the most controversial subjects (which are very often excluded by many universities). The professor must not only talk about controversial subjects (such as free speech on the campus), but must himself get involved with them, so that students may see how he actually handles an issue. If the goal of education is a sharpening of individual conscience rather than a training for socially acceptable careers, then, Sanford pointed out, it is ironical that the primary and secondary education of the brightest children today is inferior to that given to the less bright ones. The parents of bright children want them to learn what will get them to the college of their choice; they want facts poured into the children's heads, and the schools comply. The parents of less bright children, on the other hand, often are "content" to let the school concentrate on building character, developing judgment, helping the child to get the most out of life, to find meanings and values.

Ironically, many of those "well-trained" students who have learned facts and skills may find that in this fast-changing world their skills have become obsolete by automation or new discoveries by the time they are ready to start a career. On the other hand, opportunities may present themselves for which no formal education was available. To take one striking example: John Glenn's teachers could not have given him a factual education enabling him to become an astronaut because such an occupation did not exist when he was getting his basic schooling. The catalog of any major university lists a number of fields practically unknown ten years ago, such as exobiology (study of life beyond earth), bioengineering (engineering of artificial replacements of biological organs), cryogenics (study of how substances behave at extremely low temperatures), or biopsychology (the biological aspects of psychology). Yet education cannot be satisfied merely to train a student in his special field if he is to lead a meaningful life. Every person must be led to see his work as a center of self-respect, to be aware of himself in the whole picture in an expanding and changing world. He must be made to look beyond his immediate job. To give a person the feeling that he is more than part of a machine, that he is part of evolving life, education must do more than train scientists to invent more gadgets; it must train them to respond more sensitively to the meanings of life and to help make society more responsible. At the same time, education also must make those students who decide not to become scientists more familiar with science and the scientific approach to problems. It is necessary for everyone to understand what science is and what it can and cannot do, not because he may want to become a scientist but because he wants to be a responsible citizen in a world in which science has a big part. Significantly, many students returning to the universities from Peace Corps assignments demanded an education more closely related to life than to subject matter. They had discovered, from their own experience and not from tradition, what the demands and values are in today's world.

It is difficult, in the midst of the present transition period, to foresee the new values that will emerge. However, logotherapy is on firm ground with its demand for man to fall back on his own individual insights, as they are mediated by personal conscience. Personal discovery helped people in previous in-between periods overcome the uncertainties caused by crumbling traditions. Personal discovery was recommended by Socrates during his transition period. The unexamined life, he said, was not worth living. Jesus, during another transition period, castigated the "hypocritical scribes and Pharisees" for merely paying their tithe and following the letter of the law while they were, in fact, whited sepulchres "full of the bones of the dead." The Reformation, still another in-between era, shifted responsibility of personal conduct from the authority of the Church and the Pope to individual conscience. "Here I stand," Luther exclaimed. "God help me, I cannot do otherwise." Revelation, man discovered, was not restricted to Biblical times and to selected individuals; it is a continuing process and available to everyone. The emphasis shifted to the dignity and value of the individual, who was to make his own decisions. It is doubtful whether man was ready at the time of the Reformation to accept such freedom and responsibility. The question today is whether he is ready for it now.

CHAPTER VIII

The Challenge of Freedom

It is not your obligation to complete your work,
but you are not at liberty to quit.   TALMUD

MAN'S THIRST FOR FREEDOM was aroused by that fateful piece
of fruit Adam and Eve tasted, and has never been quenched.
The further we evolve away from that moment in prehistory,
the more we see how much truth and wisdom is packed into
that mythical tale, and to how many interpretations it lends
itself. As mentioned before, Frankl compares man's loss of his
instincts with the expulsion from paradise. Going one step
further, we might interpret the Fall as the original transition
period, occurring before the first set of traditions had developed — the period between the time that primeval man lost
his instinctual guidance and the time when, in his earliest
stages as a free agent, he developed his first values. That this
first freedom should manifest itself as disobedience to God,
will surprise no one who ever tasted the fruit of freedom in
any form, for freedom always establishes itself as man's
decision to say NO to authority. The child first tastes freedom
when it realizes that it can say NO to its father; the slave,
when he becomes aware that it is possible to say NO to his
master; the subject, when he discovers that he can say NO to
his king. But in every instance the newly liberated man soon
becomes aware that freedom is more than a breaking of
chains, that with emancipation the real tasks begin, that he
has lost the guardianship of the protector and the comfort of
a set of rules. Thus, early men discovered what their
descendants were to discover over and over again: that winning "freedom from" — namely, authority — is only the first
step, and that it is followed by the necessity to decide on a
"freedom to" — a commitment. Expressed in Biblical terms,

freedom to say NO to God is followed by the necessity to eat one's bread by the sweat of one's brow. In logotherapeutic terms, freedom to lead a meaningful life is followed by the acceptance of responsibility. This was true of the transition period at the dawn of man's evolution into a human being, and it is still true of the transition period of today.

Freedom in Theory and Practice

A fundamental difference exists, however, between the first and the present transition periods. The first established man's freedom on a precarious basis — one is almost tempted to say, in theory only — while today freedom has been widely won in practice. Adam found out what every child finds out at an early stage: that it has the capacity to disobey its father, but that the father has the capacity to punish. It is remarkable that early man had the awareness of his freedom when he had so little opportunity to practice it. The Jewish mystery tradition maintained that man was created for the sake of choice. It is true that Abraham had the choice to say NO to God and refuse to sacrifice his son as ordered. But who will blame Abraham for taking his son to the sacrificial altar, considering the overpowering authority of Jahweh? And who will blame Biblical man for exercising his freedom in great hesitation, fear, and trembling, after Sodom and Gomorrah, and the Flood? Who will blame historical man for cautiously feeling his way, threatened as he was by the punishment of eternal hellfire, or more immediately, by the death penalty or torture decreed by a tyrant? Yet the topic of the freedom of will has fascinated Christian writers from St. Augustine to St. Thomas Aquinas, from Calvin to Kierkegaard.

Up to modern times it required almost superhuman courage and conviction to stand up to the great weight of institutional authority. The consequences of saying NO to the Church went far beyond physical torment and death, to eternal damnation; the king, by divine right, was the absolute master on earth; in the family, the father was the Law; in the school, the schoolmaster was undisputed tyrant; for the worker, the property owners and guild masters established rigid rules. In his search for truth, the early scientist was ordered by church and state to follow a certain direction.

All this has changed. The struggle for freedom left the treatises and took to the battlefields. The Declaration of Independence was followed by a War of Independence. The struggle was joined in every field and has been won on all fronts. Western man has emancipated himself from established church and civil authority. In a chain reaction of revolutions, churchgoers have shaken off blind obedience to dogmas, citizens have overthrown the absolute monarch, slaves and women have won their emancipation, wives have achieved freedom from their husbands, children from their fathers, pupils from their teachers, workers from their employers, and scientists are allowed the freedom of unhampered discovery. One of man's oldest traditions — repressing what is frowned upon by established authority — has been shattered by religion (the priest is always right); by the state (the king is always right); by other sources of domination (father, teacher, boss-master are always right). Man's freedom is now a fact, and at the same time his life has lost meaning. For it is not the theoretical freedom that opens up in man the existential vacuum. On the contrary, theoretical freedom gives his life a content — the goal to achieve it. But once man has achieved his freedom from authority and necessity, once he has achieved independence and affluence, the danger of the existential vacuum becomes real. For the second time, man has eaten from the Tree of Knowledge and has achieved freedom actually to use that knowledge — and for the second time he has lost the shelter of the Garden. Again he is on his own, but the consequence of expulsion in this affluent and automated society is not the curse of eating his bread in the sweat of his brow, but in the boredom of his spirit. But boredom is not the only consequence of man's freedom. He also experiences guilt, because free man knows that he could have chosen otherwise, and anxiety, because the burden of freedom is great. On the other hand, freedom brings joy, because choosing is creative, and meaning, because creative activity provides reasons for meaning.

The Thrust to Unlimited Freedom

One reason that man feels unfulfilled at the very time he has finally achieved freedoms his ancestors only vaguely dreamed about, is indicated by the existential writer Albert Camus. He says that man is losing his traditional values, and then lists a few examples: music has lost melody; painting, form; poetry, rhyme and meter; thought, conviction; history, sense; and religion, God. In man's thrust toward unlimited freedom, everything has become possible because everything is permitted, and the result is anxiety and emptiness. In a group of teen-agers discussing "what is wrong with our parents," one girl complained that her parents were so permissive that she had nothing to rebel against and so couldn't find out what kind of person she was. Every youngster in that group of about thirty agreed with her. A professor of the art department at Sacramento State College observed that students, when put in front of an empty canvas, often panic and are unable to do anything. They experience the existential vacuum of the painter — no style is required, no way is pointed out to them that leads to significance, no tasks are demanded of them (as in former times when painters had patrons ordering portraits or the commemoration of important events — tasks now achieved more efficiently by photography). After the shock of the empty canvas, the professor said, the students often go back to the old masterpieces to find out what made them masterpieces, to search for significance, to reinforce values in painting.

The student panicking before the empty canvas because he has no rule to go by and is not asked to express anything but his private feelings is the prototype of modern man, sitting in front of the empty canvas of his life, free to do as he pleases. He panics. To hide his panic, he may slavishly copy old masters, or he may arbitrarily throw paint, and even garbage, on the emptiness staring at him. But filling an empty canvas with just anything is no more meaning-fulfilling than copying traditional styles. In the present universal pursuit of freedom, everyone can be a painter, poet, composer, philosopher, moralist, because anything goes. The old values have been found wanting, so all values are thrown out. This is true in all fields of expression and inquiry. In the arts, everyone expresses his own opinion unstifled by rules and conventions. In morals, pragmatists present morals as an expression of personal feelings, with no recourse to absolutes; sociologists and anthropologists stress the diversity of morals and refuse value judgments; semanticists express doubt that one man can understand another man's language; and the psychologists point to the unconscious as a reason why a man cannot even understand himself. Religion no longer inspires absolute faith. Man has placed his faith in science, but science, too, turns out to be less than an absolute master with a reliable set of rules. Science no longer is considered a source of complete truth, but rather a system of hypotheses that change as man acquires new knowledge. In mathematics, concepts of relativity are replacing the absolutes of Newton, and even axioms are no longer regarded as absolute truths but merely as arbitrary bases for postulates. In statistics, probability has replaced certainty, and physics has admitted its uncertainty principle. If physics has its uncertainty principle, what can be said about the certainty of morals?

Herein lies the danger — that each man, using his newly gained freedom, will arbitrarily develop his personal standards: his own rules in the arts, his own hypotheses in science, his own words in language, his own morality, his own set of beliefs, his own meanings. In his lunge toward freedom, man has gone on a rampage of do-it-yourself rules. If this tendency continues, and each man becomes the master builder of his own values, the world will become a modern Babel of confusion, and man's diversified, self-made morality may well lead to his self-made destruction. God's promise to Noah never again to unleash another Flood does not preclude the possibility that man himself may unlock the floodgate. Human freedom allows man to say NO even to his own existence.

The Positive Value of Freedom

Logotherapy proclaims freedom as an exclusively human quality which allows man to rise above all biological, psychological, and environmental limitations; but Frankl also warns that "man's freedom will degenerate into arbitrariness unless it is lived in terms of responsibleness." As long as man regards freedom as something merely negative, as a "freedom from" restriction, as a license to do as he pleases, there is danger that it will lead not to fulfillment, but to boredom and frustration. Proper use of freedom, Frankl says, means that we regard ourselves free to assume our own responsibleness; only then is freedom a positive value. The positive value of freedom is contained in a "freedom to" a cause or a person, in a response to a demand coming from the outside, but freely accepted. If freedom is not used in terms of responsibleness, it will not lead to meaning but, on the contrary, will add to the existential vacuum.

A perfunctory glance at how freedoms recently acquired are being used shows that this danger indeed exists. Many freedoms, gained with effort and sacrifice, are being used arbitrarily, and therefore lead to negative values. Students, fighting for their freedom of expression on the campus, use it not only to voice their political beliefs but also to voice obscenities — and they feel restless and frustrated; workers have gained not only freedom from feudal working conditions but also the freedom to paralyze industry and the public — and have lost their traditional pride in workmanship. Emancipated women have achieved not only economic and sexual equality but also their right to have their children brought up in nurseries and to divorce their husbands — and have become dissatisfied with their traditional roles as wives, mothers, and homemakers. Teen-agers are using their freedom from paternal authority to get involved in the causes they believe in but also to defy authority, and participate in violence and sex orgies — and have lost the security of being an integral and useful part of the family. The "sexual freedom leagues" springing up in many parts of the country not only fight outdated taboos and laws, but also provide complete freedom from any constraint — and have exchanged meaningful relationships for arbitrary sex. In the political area, freedom of assembly, used irresponsibly, has led to riots; freedom of speech includes the right to make a fool of oneself; and political freedom used arbitrarily — "It doesn't matter how you vote, but vote!" — has led to the election of incompetent, corrupt, or demagogic candidates, of whom Hitler was the most extreme example.

The danger of missing the positive value of freedom can be illustrated by Western man's conquest of poverty. Although, deplorably, 33 million out of 200 million Americans are still classified as "poor," for the first time in history the poor are a minority. The majority of people in the Western countries have achieved their freedom from want. How will they use this freedom? Will they go on a rampage, in their jubilation at having succeeded in overthrowing the tyranny of poverty? Will they celebrate their "freedom from" like children going through their pile of Christmas presents, unwrapping them in a hurry, playing with them for a while, and then, looking bored, throwing them on the national junk pile? Or will the "haves" of the earth widen their horizon and use their freedom from want in response to the needs of the "havenots"? Twenty years ago, at the dawn of this era of plenty, the idea of helping others was ridiculed as "giving milk to the Hottentots." Since then, American leaders have acknowledged their responsibleness through the Marshall Plan, the Peace Corps, the Poverty Program. Will individuals, in their own lives, accept similar commitments? It is, perhaps, too much to expect that man, after a million years of scarcity, should respond to the sudden outpouring from the horn of plenty with anything but grabbing; and with the predictable consequences — the existential vacuum. John Steinbeck, in an article, "What Happened to America?" wrote in the *Saturday Evening Post*, "I strongly suspect that our moral and spiritual disintegration grows out of our lack of experience with plenty." Western man has developed an economy and a technology that enable the majority, not just an aristocratic elite, to live in plenty. Not accustomed to abundance, the majority, and not just an elite, lives in boredom, frustration, and emptiness.

The Freedom Leisure Brings

The new experience with plenty extends also to the abundance of time we now have on our hands. Leisure was once the prerogative of the aristocrats, and they usually frittered it away in boredom. For the majority of a nation to have excess time is something new, and people have not yet learned how to use it. We are in somewhat the same position as our grandfathers, who built the first motor car in the shape of a horseless carriage because that was the shape they were used to. We are trying to build our first model of abundant leisure in the shape of the traditional Sabbath — a day on which man had the opportunity, in fact, the obligation — to be idle. God made the world in six days and rested on the seventh — and man was to do likewise. It became the cornerstone concept of the Protestant ethic to consider idleness a sin during the first six days, and work a sin on the seventh. The church and civil authorities codified that concept, and to this day an Englishman, for example, cannot go to the theater or see a professional soccer game on Sundays. So ingrained is this concept of leisure that some people still refuse to read fiction during the week because they consider it sinful to read, during working hours, books that are merely entertaining.

We are only beginning the era of real leisure. Automation releases 35,000 Americans from work every week, and before our young generation reaches middle age, the work week will likely have been reduced to 20 hours, and the amount of leisure increased to 100 hours. But modern technology brings about changes that go far beyond technical matters. For one thing, it makes work, which used to be a commitment, a mere job. Few people can honestly say that it would make much difference if they were replaced in their jobs by someone else, or even by a machine. This was not true of the artisan, the medieval workman, the growing child helping the mother in the home or the father on the farm. Even the slave in a pre-Civil War home was more personally needed than most employees are today. Technology made man feel superfluous in his work, and made work in many cases meaningless. But it also freed man from meaningless work and gave him leisure for tasks that can make his life meaningful.

To realize the opportunities of this gift, man will have to reverse his ideas about leisure. As long as six days a week were needed to do the work necessary for survival, the seventh was important for contemplation and spiritual refreshment. As an unintentional side effect, this arrangement drained religion, for many people, from the working days and concentrated it on Sunday only. Now, with six days of work no longer needed for survival, man must streamline the leisure model. No longer does he have to find meaning in his work for six days, and in contemplation on the seventh. He can spread meaningful activities to his leisure hours, and meaningful experiences to his working days. Man must realize that leisure is not merely absence of work, just as freedom is not merely absence of tyranny. The vacuum of nonwork has to be given content; the vacuum of meaningless work has to be given content. Contemplation and spiritual refreshment need not be crowded into Sunday, but can be spread around the leisure hours throughout the week. As man enters the era of plenty of time, he comes to the realization that Heaven could not be eternal idleness, as traditional belief has it, and he is beginning to suspect that eternal leisure may rather be the definition of hell. He is slowly learning that idleness will not fill his existential vacuum; passive watching will not fill it, nor will activity for activity's sake.

Idleness does not fill but increases man's feeling of emptiness. Frankl speaks of the "Sunday neurosis" which drives more people to suicide on their days off than on work days, when even a humdrum job fills their existence. He recalls the fact that retired people who have not filled their newly won freedom with some task tend to die shortly after their retirement.

Passive watching may bring some illusion of meaning. Television watching is probably the most popular leisure activity in the United States. Nothing is wrong with television, Frankl says, if the viewer selects the programs he likes. Television watching can bring meaning, not in the area of activity but of experience. But indiscriminate watching only deepens and does not fill the existential vacuum. Movie actress Anne Baxter, who inherited her independent thinking from her grandfather, Frank Lloyd Wright, speculated that the unrest of the bored young people of today may be caused by their treating life as if it were a continuation of television: they just sit back and let life pass by their eyes, without participation.

Activity for activity's sake is the most widespread attempt to fill one's emptiness. Young people, especially, want to be "where the action is." To many, an illusion of activity is gained by speed. They get into their car and drive — fast and aimlessly. The feverish desire to be active is not limited to youngsters. It is also widespread among the wealthy and successful, so much so that Frankl speaks of the "executive disease" that is characterized by hypertension and an inclination to coronaries, and is usually traceable to overwork. In a seminar, restricted to 24 policy-making executives in California, Frankl told of what he called "the most classical symptomatological picture of executive disease." A young Italian industrialist came to his office for a checkup. It had been established that, physically, nothing was wrong with him. During the course of the examination, Frankl asked the patient if there wasn't anything he was longing for. The patient finally admitted that there was. He already owned a private plane, but this did not satisfy him. He was therefore driving himself with overtime work so that he could afford a jet. "This patient," Frankl told his audience of executives, and his tongue was not too deeply in cheek, "was suffering most typically from executive disease: he was trying to run away from his inner void to the extent that only jet-propelled speed could help him escape."

The Private Desert

In Frankl's view, nothing is wrong with speed itself. To put the blame for man's psychological ills on the tempo of our times is, he says, "a trivial and incorrect diagnosis. Speed may cause physical illnesses and death but, psychologically speaking, our desire for speed is not a cause of illness but rather a misguided attempt to rid ourselves of our feeling of emptiness. We are trying to run away from it, and the faster the better." And he quotes a Viennese comedian who sings a little ditty, sitting on his motorcycle. Each stanza ends with the words, "I have no idea where I'm going, but I don't mind as long as I'm getting there fast."

Speeding is what Frankl terms one of man's "centrifugal" leisure activities, an attempt to escape from himself, an aimless flying off in all directions. Frankl advocates something that might be called "centripetal" leisure activities, directed toward, not away from man's center. Such activities allow man to confront himself and the existential problems he faces. Each man, Frankl says, ought to have his "private desert," some place where he can retreat to think about himself — it may be a room, a patch of grass under a tree, a cottage in the woods, a beach. Speed, in the shape of fast cars, can be used constructively to take him to his "desert." Frankl drives his car, as fast as he can and as often as he can, to his beloved Rax Mountains where he spends hours walking and rock climbing, in lonely contemplation or in company of his fellow climbers.

Many people, he feels, evade such confrontations with

themselves; they plunge into meaningless activities to run
away from their existential problems. This is the way he sees
it: During the day, their thoughts are constantly interrupted
by phone calls, secretaries, social obligations, children, and
the noises of leisure — the hi-fi, the television, the news on the
radio, the sports newscast. Then, at night they are plagued
by what he calls "existential sleeplessness"; the unfinished
thoughts do not let them fall asleep. But instead of taking
advantage of this opportunity to think through their problems, they take sleeping pills. "They fall asleep but, at the same
time, they fall prey to the repression not of the instinctual
but of the existential issues of their lives." Many people today,
Frankl says, do not have the courage to be lonely, to face and
solve their existential questions; they speed them away during
the day and tranquilize them away at night.

Responsibility and Responsibleness

To cure the Sunday neurosis, the executive disease, and
the other symptoms of the existential vacuum, logotherapy
proposes to help the patient respond to the challenges and
tasks life offers. Dr. Harvey Cushing, at the age of eighty-two,
told a friend, "The only way to endure life is always to have a
task to complete." The validity of this "prescription" has been
attested to by American Army and Navy psychiatrists, even
in extreme situations such as in North Korean and Japanese
prisoner-of-war camps and German death camps.

Man's freedom of choice, prevailing even in prisons, may
lead either to a meaningful or an empty life. To be meaningful, logotherapy asserts, life must be lived not only freely but
responsibly. The Garden of Eden was a place of blind and instinctual obedience to the law of the Creator, with no tasks
and no challenges. It was, one might say, a Garden of Non-
freedom and Nonresponsibility. When man ate the fruit, he
found himself not only free to know good and evil, but also
responsible for living with his freedom, outside the protection
of Paradise. He became the only animal that could reach out
for the good, but also the only one that could suffer from

such evils as inadequacy, discontent, unhappiness, and boredom. To avoid these negative aspects of man's humanness, he must accept this responsibleness in the three areas where he can find meaning. As Frankl puts it, each man is responsible for "what he does, whom he loves, and how he suffers."

The question has been raised: If the acceptance of responsibility is the cure for the meaningless life, why does man suffer from meaninglessness more now than in previous eras? Is man today less responsible than the Vikings, the Crusaders. or the Huns?

The answer to this question lies in logotherapy's distinction between responsibility and responsibleness. Responsibility is imposed by some authority; responsibleness is something that each individual takes upon himself. Most men, throughout history, were given responsibilities by some authority. A person's responsibilities within the family were well established — the man was the breadwinner, the woman the homemaker, the children the helpmates. The church laid down the responsibilities of the parishioners in their tightly knit parishes, providing the security of participation in the festivals and common sacraments from birth to death. The guilds demanded training and craftsmanship from their members; the schools insisted on learning and discipline from the students. In a society where freedom was restricted, and responsibility given and unquestioningly accepted, life had content. Now, man has freed himself from most outside authority; and where responsibility is not accepted from an authority, responsibleness must come from within. Responsibleness means inner discipline: each man responds not because he is forced to, but because he decides to. Traditional authorities, such as priest, king, father, or teacher, may impose responsibilities on a person, but cannot impose responsibleness, because that is the result of freedom to make one's own decisions. Responsibility without freedom is tyranny. Freedom without responsibleness is arbitrariness — this is Frankl's definition of arbitrariness — and may lead to boredom, emptiness, anxiety, and neurosis.

An incident in Frankl's life illustrates the intricate relationships among freedom, responsibility, responsibleness, and
the existential vacuum. When Frankl lectured to American
psychiatrists some years ago, one of the psychoanalysts commented that he had just returned from Moscow where he had
found a lower incidence of neurotic illnesses. He thought the
finding supported the conclusions of logotherapy because the
people behind the Iron Curtain were confronted by their
governments with immediate tasks that needed to be com-
pleted. Two years later several professors studying logotherapy during their sabbatical year in Vienna, asked Frankl
to show them the former Auschwitz concentration camp,
which is on Polish territory. The Psychiatric Association of
Krakow heard about Frankl's visit and persuaded him to talk
to them. In his improvised speech he told the Polish psychiatrists what the American psychoanalyst had told him — that in
Communist countries people are confronted with tasks and
therefore are less neurotic than Americans. When he saw several smiles in the audience, however, he added: "Well, possibly you have more tasks to complete than the Americans,
but don't forget that the Americans have retained the freedom
to choose their tasks, a freedom which is sometimes denied to
you in Poland." How wonderful a world it would be, he
concluded, to have meaningful tasks to fulfill, and also the
freedom to choose one's task according to one's own conscience!

Authority from Within

Thus "freedom from" rejects outside authority but "freedom
to" requires a self-imposed authority from within. The freedom that is established when tyranny is overthrown remains
merely license to arbitrary actions until an inner authority
takes over as a guide. At present, man finds himself in this
crucial in-between period: he no longer accepts the meaning
of life as dictated by his church, state, family, and the other
traditional institutions, and he is not yet willing to shoulder
the task of finding the direction of his life by himself.

Responsibility from above is rejected, and responsibleness from within is not yet widely accepted. Thus, man feels un-led, alone, unprotected, drifting, uprooted, and in despair.

Ours may be the most difficult transition period to over-come, but overcome we must because the consequence of failure is more severe than ever before. To borrow a phrase from the Civil Rights movement: in the slogan "We shall overcome," each of the three words is significant. We have the freedom to *overcome* the difficulties of the transition period. It is *we* who have to do the overcoming; we cannot rely on anyone else to do it for us. And we *shall* overcome, not right away, but in the future; and we need patience, determination, and will. The pursuit of meaning is the prescribed course.

Standing in the midst of one of the crucial in-between periods of history, we cannot know where our newly won free-doms will lead. We know where excess freedom often led the aristocrats. They ritualized their behavior, dress, speech, games, the right season in which to do things — and became slaves to these rituals. They also engaged in less harmless activities to keep busy. They made war, slaughtered animals for fun, risked their fortune at gambling and their lives in duels. Rarely were they ready to accept inner discipline when outer authority was gone. Will the masses do better with their freedom? The danger exists that they, too, are not ready. As Frankl formulated it recently, "the existential vacuum seems to me to issue from the twofold fact that, unlike an animal, man is not told by drives and instincts what he *must* do; nor is he, like man in former times, told by traditions and values what he *should* do. Instead, he wishes to do what other people do, or he does what other people wish him to do; in other words, he succumbs to either conformism or totalitarianism."

We may add that, in either case, the freedom won in the American and French revolutions will be lost again. For the great aims of these revolutions vanish not only when man succumbs to dictators, but also where he surrenders to con-formity. A society to which one conforms does not promote

freedom, only equality. Personal liberty, Frankl says, is sacri-
ficed for an impersonal equality, and fraternity degenerates
into a mere herd instinct.

Man may renounce his freedom in still another way. He
may abandon the freedom he won from church and state
authorities and accept the slavery of scientific authority. After
having rejected predetermination on religious grounds, he
accepts it on scientific grounds. He feels determined by his
genes, his glands, his drives, his emotions, his early childhood
experiences, his environment, his economic conditions, and
the God of Science knows what else. But logotherapy asserts
that, in spite of all these scientifically established limitations,
man retains an important core area of freedom that no one
can take from him except he himself, by not using it. Logotherapy encourages man to use his freedom, and use it responsibly lest, like the sorcerer's apprentice, he become the
slave of his own scientific creation.

A Feverish Search

But the prospect is bright that man, as before, will successfully cross the transition period and arrive at new values. We
do not have an individual spokesman of the new age, such as
Jesus was at the transition period of Antiquity, who spoke of a
new world where values would change to such an extent that
"many who are first now will be last then." No *one* person is
speaking in those terms, but many of our young men and
women are in feverish search for values that will fit the future. They have no particular ideology; they are against
capitalism, communism, and all other isms, which they reject
as part of the thinking of the old generation and of an ethic
that has become identified with the conventional side. They
do not want to do things because they "ought" to do them
or are "expected" to do them; they want to find their own
individual motives for their actions. They do not want merely
to study history, but to participate in it. They are not content
to hear about a social order handed down to them from
their ancestors but want to discover and shape a new order

with which to experiment; each lonely individual for himself. They protest against a multitude of things — the war in Vietnam, sexual taboos, conformity in clothing, early curfews, restrictions on the campus, puritanical parents, windbag political orators — and behind all these protests they are searching for a new philosophy. They mistrust the older generation and its values; they look at conformity as the poverty of the spirit, and reject any kind of outside authority. They strive for individualism and, to gain identity, oppose all standards of their traditional society.

Theirs is a new kind of rebellion. The revolutions of the past dealt with political and economic exploitation, and these are still fought by the people in Africa, Asia, Latin America, and by the Negroes in the United States. But they are revolutions most of the West has already won. America's social conflicts revolve around issues which ultimately boil down to questions of the meaning of life.

This rebellion in the West also goes far beyond the traditional revolt of youth against their parents; it is directed against society. And for the first time in history it is waged, not against a society that offers poverty, hunger, and depression, but against an affluent society. The revolution of the West is staged by people who have won their "freedom from" want and authority, and are fighting a "freedom to" revolution: to find new ideals and values to which to dedicate themselves. They have an abundance of material goods, but they do not want to pay their elders' price of compromises and double standards, which they see as the consequence of an adherence to outdated values. They are looking for some overarching principles that their parents did not find.

One can see examples of this rebellion in newspapers, books, and on television screens. An angry young rebel complained in a letter to the *San Francisco Chronicle* about a generation that "spends 20 billion a year to pulverize a few hamlets on the other side of the globe while our own cities fall to pieces in neglect"; that "spends billions to put a man in a capsule in outer space while millions down here have antiquated and dangerous transportation"; that "trains our healthy 18-year-olds to kill and be killed while maintaining laws against 'taking the life' of an unborn embryo that doctors feel may be born deformed." A civil rights worker, a student, is quoted in *Sex and the College Student* as sneering at the

> pompous, self-righteous (college) officials, noisy with worry about orgasm in young people, but discreetly silent when we are sent off to war to kill or be killed; full of reminders about how moral we must be, and responsible to others . . . but without a word of concern about the immorality of slums next door, or the dishonest intrigue we've practiced in the Caribbean or elsewhere. . . . If I wear a beard and a girl I love stays in my room all night and I sleep with her, I'm a beatnik and in a state of moral decline. If I shave and go to a whorehouse, buy stocks on the South African exchange that net me a large profit, and sign up for the CIA when I graduate from college, my behavior is unquestioned and my integrity assumed. . . . We're immature and demanding, they say. We'll grow up, they reassure themselves. What they mean by grow up is give up — to sell out, acquiesce, and morally die.[1]

The rebel generation denies that it is immoral. It claims, on the contrary, that it is the Establishment that is immoral and that they, the youth, are developing an emerging ethic that will fit the present. A portrait of American youth is given by two University of California sociologists, J. L. Simmons and Barry Winograd, in *It's Happening*. The rebels of today, they say, do not give automatic allegiance to such cornerstones of conventional society as Christianity, "my country right or wrong," the sanctity of marriage and premarital chastity, civil obedience, the accumulation of wealth, the right and even competence of parents, schools, and the government to make decisions for everyone. They reject the charge that they, the young, are violent, irresponsible, sex- and dope-crazy. "Look at you," they tell their elders, "blowing up whole countries for the sake of some crazy ideology that you don't live up to anyway." They denounce the Establishment for brainwashing "a whole generation of kids into getting a revolving charge account and buying your junk." They taunt their elders with needing stiff drinks before "you have the balls to talk to another human being," with "making it with your neighbor's wife on the sly just to try and prove that you're really alive," with being "hooked on *your* cafeteria of pills . . . and screwing up the land and the water and the air for profit."[2]

The rebels refuse to take their parents' values for granted; they insist on experiencing life themselves, accept no advice based on someone else's experience, but take the risks of following their own conscience.

A New Morality

This courting of raw experience, say Simmons and Winograd, gives many people the impression that the young are without any morals whatsoever; that they are selfishly pursuing swift gratification of their impulses. But, the two sociologists point out, the young are simply following another, different set of standards, a new emerging ethic which they call the "hang-loose" ethic because it "hangs a bit loose from traditional Americana."

But indications are that the ethic of the young will win out over traditional Americana. The young always have a way of winning out over the old. *Time* magazine with its scent for things to come, made the generation of twenty-five and under the "Man of the Year" 1966, in preference to old-generation leaders such as President Johnson, De Gaulle, or Mao Tsetung. The *Time* editors predict that the young "will infuse the future with a new sense of morality, a transcendent and contemporary ethic that could infinitely enrich the 'empty society.'" And the editors also observe that the new generation has "a keen ability to sense meaning on many levels at the same time."

It is too early to say whether the emerging ethic is going to lead to an individualized ethic of the future, or to a morass of lawlessness, but it is certain that it is the consequence of man's successful struggle to gain freedom in all fields. Freedom gives people the license to be immoral but also the opportunity to achieve true morality which is based, as Frankl points out, on man's *decision* to be moral. Today, man's motivation to be moral is shifting from the fear of the consequences, such as hellfire, witch-hunt trials, tarring and feathering, and the fatherly rod, to inner judgment. Only a generation ago, a young man was "moral" because he was afraid of venereal diseases, and a young girl because she was afraid of becoming pregnant. Now, in the age of antibiotics and the pill, young people — if they are moral — will have to be moral because they decide to be. Individual conscience speaks up, and it does not always speak the language of tradition. A druggist in Columbus, Ohio, refuses to sell cigarettes, and gives out antismoking leaflets instead, pointing out that he is in the business to improve the community's health. "I'd be a hypocrite," he says, "if I would sell people cigarettes, an item proven harmful to health."

The German writer of the Enlightenment, Gotthold Ephraim Lessing, said two hundred years ago that he wished there were men in every country who are beyond the "superstition of nationalism" and knew exactly where patriotism ceases to be a virtue. We have come to that point. Not only youthful rebels doubt the wisdom of blind nationalism. Richard Cardinal Cushing, the Roman Catholic Archbishop of Boston, said, "Let America realize that self-scrutiny is not treason, self-examination is not disloyalty. Patriotism is not a cloak for the blanket and blind acceptance of all decisions made by the United States. This is not patriotism. It can be, instead, the road to national disintegration."[3] In spite of the recent upsurge of nationalism — especially virulent in Lessing's own country — there are individuals in many countries who realize not only where patriotism ceases to be a virtue, but also the limitations of such other unquestioned virtues as mother love and religion. Psychologists have helped us see how long relying on our mother is of value, and at what point this reliance begins to become a liability. Philosophers (and even theologians) have taught us to distinguish between a religion that helps the individual reach out for the highest dimension of human existence, and a religion that is used by the Establishment as "opium of the people."

The new morality puts all institutions, traditions, and their slogans under the microscope. The young generation does not automatically assume that a gentlemen's agreement is made by gentlemen; that the white man's burden is a burden for the white man; or that national honor is honorable under all circumstances. The rebels do not accept assumptions just because they worked in the past. The saying that "the people know best" was true for building a local school, but no longer holds for deciding what to do in outer space. The right to bear arms was an important constitutional right in pioneer days, but now more people are killed accidentally by private firearms than homes are protected by them. The two-party system presented a valid choice between two contrasting ideologies before the industrial revolution, but such a contrast today exists mostly in people's minds. Abortion laws were "moral" at a time when a high birth rate was an economic necessity but have become "immoral" in an era of overpopulation. A competitive society, with its repressed aggressiveness, was an incentive to progress in an empty country in a wide-open world, but is a danger in a pressure-cooker world armed with nuclear bombs. Freedom once meant the storming of the Bastille but it now means the opening of our homes and offices and schools to the excluded because, as the young rebels realize, freedom is denied not only to those who are locked in but also to those who are locked out. The young generation is not overly interested in the ideologies their fathers still take terribly seriously. Socialism, free enterprise, states' rights, the welfare state, or the cold war are much less serious problems to the young than to their elders. The young people of today do not think that life can be lived meaningfully according to rationally developed ideas based on old models, but only according to existential concepts.

The Choices of Freedom

The choice, then, is to give up the newly won freedoms as too dangerous, or to risk the unknown. We can retreat to dependency, conformity, totalitarianism. We can submit to the machine, to the tyranny of drives and other psychological forces, to the dictatorship of power for power's sake. Or we can go forward and accept the widening of responsibleness that comes with freedom: the creative use of leisure, the acceptance of "out-groups" as part of our responsibility, the emphasis on individual and existential living. This is the direction in which the youth of today are going, to the distress and bafflement of their elders. Young people stress each individual's right to lead his life as he sees fit, to grow a beard, to dress any way he feels comfortable, to spend his time as he wants to — painting, writing, talking, listening to records, taking LSD, making love all day. Work no longer is a virtue, and idleness no longer is a sin. On the contrary, meaningful leisure activity is a virtue and moonlighting is a sin because, for the first time, work is in short supply. Thus, the young people do not look for a job for the sake of working or earning money. "We got plush jobs," a student said upon graduation, "but they use only part of us. We want to participate wholly, we want to be meaningfully employed in work that engages everything in us, also our mind and spirit, we want to be a community of men to love and be loved."

This may sound visionary to people over thirty, but to the young it is reality as they see it. These young revolutionaries use a vocabulary different from that of the men who made the traditional revolutions. They do not talk about "justice" and "equality" but about love, companionship, communication, relationship, and participation. They want to be "with it," part of the whole. They struggle for the freedom *to* something: to live up to the best in themselves; to get involved; to care; to listen to their conscience.

The revolution of the young may seem a small movement, centered in college communities, high schools, and civil rights groups. But the young generation that is breaking away from the old is gradually receiving the support of the universities (which are to serve the young); the big corporations (which hire the young); the churches (which must appeal to the young to survive); and the government (which must have the votes of the young). Youth is the largest minority in the United States, and may soon become a majority — the average age of the voter is estimated to be 27 years, and going down. Sooner or later they will take charge of the Establishment and become the lawmakers. The decision will be theirs: whether to "run scared" of their freedom, or to use it to alter existing institutions and values, and to build a society based on cooperation, mature acceptance of sex, death, world citizenship, respect for the here and now, and the realities of the twentieth century. Theirs will not be a popular decision. Americans, obsessed with happy endings, will have to realize that they are in many situations for which no happy ending is possible, and that many endings will be disagreeable because they will call for vast changes in the *status quo*. A new set of laws will have to enshrine the new values, but conceivably the time will come when man will, by his own choice, extend his concern beyond his immediate in-group, nation, even culture; when no law will be needed to tell him to share his neighborhood with men of different skin color, his food with people of different nationality, and even different systems of government, and when conscience will tell a man to respond to a demand of reality even if it goes against his needs and instincts. For example, he may respond to the reality of pollution by voluntarily foregoing personal profit and entertainment to keep water and air clean. Or he may respond to the reality of overpopulation by keeping the number of his children to two, or by having no children at all if he carries a genetic defect. Freedom will come when man is willing to restrain his own freedom for the sake of others, and justice will come when those who are not hurt by injustice are as indignant as those who are.

This sounds utopian, but we must remember that even

utopias are subject to change. Man's present transition period may lead into an era where utopias no longer are the product of conceptual thinking but will become, to some extent at least, existential. Existential utopias are not seen as an all-at-once vision, but are experienced as a step-by-step reality, and have their limitations, of which we are becoming increasingly aware. We know that it is biologically impossible to breed perfect humans, but we do know how to eliminate some defects. We know that it is instinctually impossible for the lamb to lie down with the lion but we also know that two men who have achieved their freedom from want can live in peace with each other because men can rise above their instincts. We know that it is socially impossible for man to live in an ant-like society, but we also know that man can learn to organize work with ant-like precision in order to have more leisure for human-like creativity.

Man has been thinking and preaching about utopias long enough. He knows what he "ought" to do, but he may be entering an era that gives him the freedom actually to pursue what he thinks is right, without direction from institutions still geared to the values of yesterday. But directions he must have, and they must come from within. That is why Frankl, to his American audiences, often suggests that they ought to supplement their Statue of Liberty on the East Coast by a Statue of Responsibleness on the West Coast. The torch that directs the "poor (and) . . . huddled masses" toward freedom must be reinforced by an inner light that directs them toward a meaningful use of their liberty, or the land of the free may become a land of the frustrated.

CHAPTER IX

Mental Health in a Time of Transition

People tell me I oversimplify. . . . They overcomplicate.

DR. ERIC BERNE

WHEN VALUES ARE QUESTIONED and standards no longer are clear-cut, people feel lost. Without traditions to guide him, the individual must find other bases for making choices. His house no longer is built on rock. Or, if it is, the rock is not what it used to be. Physicists have discovered that it consists mostly of empty space and swirling electrons; astronomers say that the rock we call our home is but a tiny speck in an expanding universe; philosophers claim that the world of thought has moved along swiftly and left the rock behind. The individual is thrown upon his own resources.

Fortunately, the sciences, which have done much to undermine man's confidence in traditional values, can also help him reassess himself. What are the forces that motivate man? Can they be controlled? To what extent? In what areas? Is man feeling guilty about things over which he has no control, while refusing responsibility for things over which he has? What kind of creature is he? What is his "normal" behavior? When does he possess mental health, and when is he sick? How can the therapist prevent and cure such sickness? What is the role of the therapist in this period of transition? Is he to make it easy for the patient to adjust to the shifting values of today, or redirect him to find new standards and anchoring places for his rope, something to hold onto and perhaps even to climb up on?

The Emphases of Logotherapy

Logotherapy does not claim to have found the answers to these questions; nor is it the only school of therapy trying to find answers. It moves in a definite direction, however — away from adjustment, and toward individual responsibility. It emphasizes mental health rather than mental disease, total man rather than the psyche only, man's freedom rather than his limitations; values that beckon rather than drives that push; the challenges of the future rather than the traumas of the past.

That Frankl's ideas have moved into the mainstream of advanced American thinking was indicated in a symposium held in St. Louis, Missouri, in 1965, entitled "The Challenge (to Psychiatry) of the Next Ten Years" and sponsored by the American Psychiatric Association.[1] The moderator, Howard P. Rome, a psychiatrist at the Mayo Clinic, stressed the revolution in psychiatry that is taking place in this "age of revolutionists." Huston Smith, professor of philosophy at MIT, listed man's crisis in values as a major reason for needed changes in psychiatry. He pointed out that the shifting of mores within a single lifetime deprives the individual of objective anchors for his values, and forces him to build, existentially, his own moral standards.

The new tasks of therapy were outlined by Nevitt Sanford, in his capacity as Director of Stanford University's Institute for the Study of Human Problems. Psychiatry, he said, must not be satisfied merely with curing diseases, but must also help prevent them. It must build strength in individuals so that they can better cope with the stresses of modern life. Psychiatry must consider the total person and must be guided by "a conception of what we want people to become . . . and (what they) should become. It must consider the value of individual development in relation to other values" and must give attention to what is being done to develop our citizens. Preventive therapy, Huston Smith added, must be more than a "gatekeeper" watching out for early symptoms and prescribing early treatments. It must find out what segments of the population are particularly prone to mental illness and under what conditions, and where the high risks, the predictable stresses are. He mentioned the Peace Corps as an example of how psychiatric services may be used preventively to anticipate and deal with emotional problems which volunteers are likely to meet not only in their assignment abroad, but also on reentering their own culture.

Logotherapy meets many of these challenges to mental health in this era of transition, and meets them on a philosophical as well as on a medical level. No therapy can exist without its own views about the nature of man. Such has been the case with all major therapies including that of Freud, as was stated by one of his greatest disciples, Paul Schilder. Often the philosophy underlying the therapy has been more important than the therapy itself.

This has been strikingly true of psychoanalysis. Sigmund Freud, a medical doctor, set out to find cures for the diseases of the mind. Yet, one generation after Freud's death, his discoveries have revolutionized not only medicine but also, at least in the United States, practically all aspects of human life — our education and child rearing, our politics, our leisure activities, our marriage relationships, our laws, our prisons, our writing and literary criticism, our sales techniques. In fact, a good case can be made that the influence of Freud in each of these areas far outweighs that in medicine. More people have been prompted to buy goods, elect political candidates, and write and read books through application of Freud's findings than have been cured by psychoanalysis. Freud's contribution to the understanding of our healthy self and our relationships with others (parents, spouses, children, voters, customers, pupils, employees) is spectacular. His contribution to the curing of the sick is less striking when compared with medical advances in other fields during the same period — for example, the advances in antibiotics or new techniques in surgery. It is startling to realize that Freud's contribution to mental health lies largely in fields outside medicine, and is based on his view of man. Through Freud's influence man has become consciously aware of forces within himself that motivate his actions, feelings, and thoughts; and this awareness has helped him retain and recover his mental health.

Other therapies have refined man's self-understanding by

drawing attention to such varied areas as his will to power, his influence through society, his religious roots, and his meaning orientation. All these schools of therapy contributed to mental health at least as much by their life philosophies as by their medical techniques. This is also true of logotherapy. In fact, Frankl was so conscious of the importance of a *Weltanschauung* that, after receiving his medical degree, developing his logotherapy, and testing it existentially in a world of economic crisis, death camps, and postwar despair, he went back to the University of Vienna to receive a doctor's degree in philosophy.

Among the five aspects of logotherapy he lists as contributing to mental health, three belong to the field of philosophy, and two more strictly to the field of medicine. The three philosophical concepts concern the interpretation of personal existence, the combating of collective neuroses, and the comforting of incurables. The two medical aspects deal with the treatment of neuroses specifically originating in man's noös (spirit), and with neuroses of a different nature for which logotherapy has proved helpful.

Interpreting Personal Existence

Logotherapy contributes to mental well-being through its interpretation of personal existence, but it is not the therapist who is doing the interpreting. Frankl conceives the role played by a logotherapist not as that of a painter, who presents "the world as he sees it," but rather as that of an eye specialist who helps the patient "see the world as it is."

This effort to help man see the world (including himself) as it is goes back to Socrates, who counseled, "Know thyself," and to Jesus, who knew that the truth will make us free. Freud specified that knowledge of ourselves must include the truth hidden in our unconscious, and went on to define the core of the self as "the obscure id" which is governed by the pleasure principle. Frankl shifts the emphasis from the psyche to the noös and sees the core of the self in the will to meaning. Through this emphasis, logotherapy counteracts recent developments that deprive the concept of man of its human dimension and threaten to reduce man to a thing, to a product of the forces within and around himself.

Reductionism begins with the claims of biologists that man is a form of computer; the findings of psychoanalysts that man is a battleground of clashing ids, egos, and superegos; and the statements of sociologists that man is the outcome of his environment. According to Frankl all these statements are legitimate: man *is* a computer, a battleground of psychological forces, and the outcome of his environment. But he is also infinitely more. Reductionism becomes harmful when it leads man to believe that he is *nothing but* a computer, a battleground, and an outcome, disregards his entire human dimension, and reduces him to a subhuman level. Frankl defines reductionism as a new kind of nihilism — a belief, not in "nothingness" but in "nothingbutness."

It is important for a person's mental health that he remain convinced that he houses authentic phenomena and motivations. He must trust, for instance, in his capacity to experience genuine love that comes from his own human dimension, and is not merely either a reaction formation concealing hostility or "nothing but" a sublimation of sex. He must believe that he possesses a genuine conscience which is not merely the result of parental punishment. Man must become convinced anew that love, conscience, art, religion, and his desire for truth and meaning are authentic phenomena and not just sublimations, repressions, and defense mechanisms. Yet, reductionism has become widespread among people who have gained a smattering of psychology through popular books, articles, and movies, and it is still promoted by analysts of the orthodox school. Frankl quotes Lawrence J. Hatterer, a New York psychiatrist, as saying that "many an artist has left the psychiatrist's office enraged by interpretations that he writes because he is an injustice collector or a sadomasochist; that he acts because he is an exhibitionist; that he dances because he wants to seduce his audience sexually; or that he paints to overcome strict bowel training by free smearing."

Freud himself traced Leonardo da Vinci's interest in paint-

ing madonnas to a sublimation for the artist's longing for his
mother from whom he had been separated at an early
age. Calvin Hall in *A Primer of Freudian Psychology* (p. 82)
adds that various psychologists have regarded Shakespeare's
sonnets, Whitman's poetry, Tschaikowsky's music, and
Proust's novels as sublimations of homosexual yearnings.
K. R. Eissler's two-volume work on Goethe, a psychoanalyti-
cal study, follows the same reductionist interpretation. Julius
Heuscher published a review of that work in the Fall 1964
issue of the *Journal of Existentialism:*

> Eissler portrays to us a genius (Goethe) with the earmarks
> of a manic-depressive, paranoid, and epileptoid-disorder, of
> homosexuality, incest, voyeurism, exhibitionism, fetishism,
> impotence, narcissism, obsessive compulsive neurosis, hys-
> teria, megalomania, etc. . . . Eissler seems to focus almost
> exclusively on the instinctual dynamic forces that underlie
> the artistic product. . . . Gradually we are led to believe
> that "Goethe-Faust" and their work are but the results of
> pregenital fixations. Their struggle [the reviewer concluded]
> does not really aim for an ideal, for beauty, for value, but for
> the overcoming of an embarrassing problem of premature
> ejaculation.

Where this kind of reductionism can lead is indicated by
the California sociologist, William Irwin Thompson, who
wrote in a 1962 issue of *Main Currents in Modern Thought:*
"If the most educated members of our culture continue to
look at geniuses as disguised sexual perverts, if they think that
all values are . . . specious fictions, . . . how can we be
alarmed if the mass of our culture shows little regard for
values and instead loses itself in an orgy of consumption,
crime, and immorality."

Although psychiatrists often are trapped into reductionist
thinking, the man in the street has no difficulty in accepting
logotherapy's interpretation of personal existence because it
checks with his day-by-day experience: that man's reaching
for meaning, truth, beauty, and love is an authentic human
phenomenon.

Combating Collective Neurosis

Logotherapy also applies its philosophy to combat certain "collective neuroses" of our times. Actually, Frankl doubts that the present is an age of any greater anxiety than were the times of the Migration of Nations, the Black Death, the witch hunts, or other periods of stress. Nevertheless, if one can speak at all of a collective neurosis today as a basis for the spreading feeling of meaninglessness, it has four symptoms, which are enumerated in *The Doctor and the Soul* and discussed more fully in *Psychotherapy and Existentialism*.

Briefly, they are provisional living, fatalism, collective thinking, and fanaticism. Provisional living, a day-to-day attitude, is caused by fear of nuclear war, which keeps people from engaging in meaningful encounters and making long-range commitments and, instead, encourages the quick "use" of people and the pursuit of short-range goals such as superficial pleasures. Fatalism denies the individual the freedom to make responsible decisions — he thus considers himself a product of outer circumstances and inner conditions beyond his control. Collective thinking deprives a person of his own choices because he accepts the decisions of the masses. Fanaticism, finally, makes the individual not only accept the choices made by others, but also allow himself to be ruled by them. "The fanatic," says Frankl, "does not have an opinion; the opinion has him."

Frankl finds provisional living and fatalism more prevalent in the democracies, collective thinking and fanaticism in the totalitarian states. All four symptoms are caused by a refusal to accept personal responsibleness and they encourage the existential vacuum. A person cannot find individual meaning if he does not believe that it is worth finding, or thinks it is impossible to find, or accepts someone else's meanings as his own. Logotherapy combats this feeling of hopelessness by stressing that a person's life does have a meaning, and that it is up to him to find it.

Comforting the Sufferers

The third area in which logotherapy's world view is helpful is in existential conflicts, and especially in cases of unavoidable suffering. This aspect, too, is covered in *The Doctor and the Soul,* which presents the guiding principles of logotherapy and its application to what Frankl calls "medical ministry, this no-man's land between medicine and religion." To comfort the sufferer has always been the task of the minister as well as of the physician. Today it is harder than ever to know whether help for a person's suffering should come from the field of religion or of medicine. Frankl pleads for cooperation between the minister and the psychiatrist, although their aims are different: "The minister aims at salvation, the psychiatrist at mental health." As Frankl put it in the introduction of his *The Doctor and the Soul:*

> The goal of psychotherapy is to heal the soul, to make it healthy; the aim of religion is something essentially different — to save the soul. But the side-effect of religion is an eminently psycho-hygienic one. Religion provides man with a spiritual anchor, with a feeling of security such as he can find nowhere else. But, to our surprise, psychotherapy can produce an analogous, unintended side-effect. For although the psychotherapist is not concerned with helping his patient to achieve a capacity of faith, in certain felicitous cases the patient regains his capacity for faith.

Logotherapy's contribution to comforting those suffering existentially, and particularly those suffering hopelessly, has been discussed in Chapter III. Frankl has shown that the meaning of life is not measured in terms of years lived (no more than the significance of a book is measured by the number of its pages); that life can be made meaningful retroactively even during the last hours; and, most importantly, that life's deepest and ultimate meaning can often be perceived under circumstances when no help is available, when life has been stripped of all nonessentials.

In addition to these often-stated contributions of logotherapy to the relief of suffering, one other point needs to be
mentioned: the doctor-patient relationship. Every patient —
the *homo patiens,* to quote the title of one of Frankl's untranslated books — is by definition a sufferer, and as such,
entitled not only to the physician's technical know-how, but
also to his sympathetic understanding. One of my childhood
recollections is that my grandmother saw her family doctor
once a week and received great comfort from his listening
to her complaints. Today I am grateful for the magnificent
annual multiphasic checkup I am getting in my hospital,
where I am handed, for three hours, from nurse to nurse and
from machine to machine, following twenty phases listed on
a printed sheet, while I am asked to answer 150 questions on
flash cards, to be handled by a computer. I know that I am
getting incomparably better medical care than my grandmother did, but something has become lost in the "progress."
That this something is also missing in much of psychotherapy
is evident from many of the written questions Frankl receives
after his lectures. Many deal with the impersonal treatment
of the patients by therapists. "Why does the American psychiatrist never advise or direct his patient?" reads a typical
question. "He merely listens, coldly, silently." In contrast,
the logotherapist is a participating partner in the common
effort to find relief. He does not merely hold up a mirror in
which the patient can see his past; he discusses the present
in order to reorient the patient toward a world of meanings
to fulfill. Gerald F. Kreyche, professor of philosophy at De
Paul University, speculated that "the incredible attempts to
dehumanize man at the concentration camps of Auschwitz and
Dachau led Frankl to commence the humanization of psychiatry through logotherapy."

Abraham Maslow, in his *Religions, Values, and Peak Experiences,* points to the I-Thou encounter between the existential psychotherapist and his patient that the mirror-type
analyst cannot achieve. "Even the classical psychoanalysts
would now be willing to admit," Maslow says, "that care, con-

cern, and agapean love for the patient are implied by the analyst in order that therapy may take place."

But this doctor-patient encounter is not enough. As Frankl explains in *Psychotherapy and Existentialism,* logotherapy goes one step further and opens that two-sided relationship to include a third "partner" — meaning. The doctor helps the patient to open the door toward meaning. Speaking at the International Congress of Psychotherapy in Barcelona, Spain, Frankl pointed out that logotherapy is more than analysis; it is therapy. It is more than ontoanalysis, analysis of being; it is, as its name implies, "logo"-therapy, therapy through meaning.

Therapy of Noögenic Neuroses

As a medical treatment, logotherapy is specifically indi- cated in cases of noögenic neuroses — neuroses rooted in the human dimension of the noös. The philosophical basis for such illnesses, which are often value clashes and conflicts of conscience, has already been stated, and the medical aspects lie beyond the scope of this book.

A few points of general interest, however, need to be made. One, mentioned before, is logotherapy's assertion that mental disease may originate in the patient's body (caused by the malfunctioning of a gland, for instance), his psyche (caused, for example, by a childhood trauma), or his noös (caused, perhaps, by a value conflict). Therefore, a psychiatrist is required to make a diagnosis based on the *totality* of the patient. In pre-Freudian times all diseases were believed to be caused physically; the Freudian discoveries tempted many analysts to suspect the psyche as the single source of mental illness. Frankl is careful not to fall into a similar trap and claim that all mental sickness is triggered in the noös. The first step, therefore, is to determine the area in which the sick- ness originated. Logotherapy alone will not cure a neurosis caused by a chemical deficiency in the body, and psycho- analysis will not cure an existential neurosis. Edwin G. Bor- ing, professor of psychology at Harvard, describes the futility of psychoanalysis in dealing with his own case of existential neurosis, in an article, "Was This Analysis a Success?"[2] He had felt depressed because his professional accomplishments seemed to be waning and the future looked "utterly intolerable." He went, as a patient, through 168 sessions of psychoanalysis, with no improvement. Analysis could not help him because his depression was not based on anything that had happened in his past, but on his current existential despair.

Frankl has recorded cases in which all three dimensions of the patient — his body, his psyche, and his noös — were implicated in a neurosis. One of these patients, a schoolteacher, suffered from severe depressions. They were diagnosed as being caused organically, and an appropriate drug was prescribed. But the depression also had a psychological cause: she was depressed over her depressions; her immediate condition was but a psychological reaction to something that originally had been an organic defect. In therapeutic sessions she was instructed to avoid brooding as much as possible because such brooding would understandably but unjustifiably magnify her bleak views. Frankl suggested to her to let the depression pass by her as the cloud passes the sun: the sun exists behind the cloud even if we cannot see it for the moment. Such therapy released much that was unlocked in the patient, but also disclosed her existential distress: her low opinion of herself as a person whom fate had hopelessly handicapped with recurring depressions. Here logotherapy in the strict sense of the word was indicated. Frankl convinced her that what matters is the attitude people take toward their unchangeable fate, that her depressions posed a challenge for her. She could decide to shape her life in spite of the difficulties that had developed. In time the patient learned to see her life as full of personal tasks, in spite of the depressions. Indeed, the depressions presented an additional task: that of living with them, of overcoming them instead of being crushed by them. The patient led a life "more conscious of responsibility and more filled with meaning than before

treatment — more so, probably, than if she had never fallen
ill and never needed treatment." She later wrote Frankl, "I
was not a human being until you made me one," which
prompted him to recall a sentence by Goethe, "If we take
people as they are, we make them worse. If we treat them as
if they were what they ought to be, we help them become
what they are capable of becoming." Frankl considers this
sentence "the finest maxim for any kind of psychotherapy."

Logotherapy sometimes is blamed for being "too direc-
tive," telling people what to do and what to believe. Frankl,
however, teaches again and again that meaning must be found
by the patient, and cannot be given, least of all by the therapist. He jokingly remarked that no one expects Freudian
analysis (which is concerned with sex) to arrange for marriage partners, and no one expects individual psychology
(which is concerned with power) to arrange for positions of
employment. Likewise, logotherapy (which is concerned with
meaning) does not arrange for the patient's meaning. As
Frankl points out, logotherapy widens the patient's vision so
that he can become aware of the full spectrum of meaning
potentials, and of the fact that life never ceases to hold a
meaning for every person, literally to his last breath.

Therapy of Psychogenic Neuroses

Although logotherapy is especially indicated in noögenic
neuroses, it also proves helpful for psychogenic neuroses —
those originating in the patient's psyche. Two techniques for
such cases, developed by Frankl and generally used by logotherapists, are paradoxical intention and de-reflection.

Paradoxical intention is applicable with phobic and obsessive-compulsive patients. It uses what Frankl calls "the unique
human quality of self-detachment," which enables man to
step away from himself, look at himself from the outside, oppose himself, even laugh at himself. Man's capacity for self-
detachment manifests itself not only in the "defiant power of
the human spirit" but also in his sense of humor. Paradoxical

intention, one might say, enables the patient to laugh his neurosis away, while de-reflection enables him to ignore his symptoms.

De-reflection is useful with patients showing a compulsion to reflect too much on themselves, as in most sexual neuroses. It employs another human quality, what Frankl calls "man's capacity of self-transcendence," which enables man to forget about himself and reach out beyond himself, toward other human beings and toward meanings.

According to a definition given by Frankl at the Symposium on Logotherapy in London and published in the *American Journal of Psychotherapy* in 1966, by paradoxical intention "the patient is encouraged to do, or wish to happen, the very things he fears." The objective of this drastic cure is to break the vicious circle that has developed as the result of anticipatory anxiety. The patient, for whatever reason, has developed a fear — for example, of open places. Every time he approaches an open place he becomes fearful, not only of the open place but also of being afraid, and specifically of the consequences of his fear — a collapse, a stroke, a heart attack. Paradoxical intention aims at breaking that pattern, even if only for a moment, so that the patient can see himself not as the helpless victim of his fate but as its master. This moment is the dramatic turning point of the patient's sickness, and is also the hardest for the patient to face and for the doctor to bring about. Here the patient's sense of humor is helpful. The logotherapist may tell the patient, "Now you run out into the street and have yourself a heart attack — why, it's early in the morning, you still have time for three heart attacks, and throw in a little stroke while you're at it." If the patient then smiles, a first victory is won. As Gordon W. Allport of Harvard has observed, "The neurotic who learns to laugh at himself may be on the way to self-management, perhaps to cure."[3] In some cases the patient will try paradoxical intention because he has nothing to lose. In other cases he will implore the therapist not to send him into the street. In either case the patient is likely to come back relieved — even when he was certain the therapy would fail. The therapist, of course, can send the phobic patient out only after a careful diagnosis. So long as the patient really believes that he has a heart condition, the doctor cannot use paradoxical intention. He first must convince the patient, deep inside, that his anxiety is neurotic.

Paradoxical intention is practiced at clinics in Europe, North and South America, Africa, and Japan. Hans O. Gerz, clinical director of the Connecticut Valley Hospital, reported on a six-year study of 51 patients, almost 90 percent of whom recovered or improved considerably after application of paradoxical intention.[4] Time of recovery was rapid. Patients who had been sick for several years were usually cured within one year, acute cases responded within four to twelve sessions. The patients were encouraged to continue using the technique themselves until, as Gerz puts it, "the paradoxical intention strangles the symptoms."

The briefness of the therapy and the attention to strangling the symptoms rather than to uncovering the causes has aroused doubt in some psychiatric circles — unfounded, as thirty years of experience show. Today, most psychiatrists have come to recognize that length of treatment does not necessarily equate with lasting results, and the fear that eliminated symptoms will turn up elsewhere has proved unfounded. The attention of many psychiatrists to causes rather than symptoms prompted the late William Menninger to observe that it was not absolutely necessary to know the cause of a fire in order to extinguish it.

In de-reflection, the second major technique used by logotherapists, the patient learns to bypass himself and the symptoms of his neurosis, and to focus instead on other human beings to encounter and on meanings to fulfill. According to Frankl, 90 percent of impotence or frigidity is caused by the patient's concentration on himself and his lack of potency or orgasm.

Here, too, a pattern develops that has to be broken, and again it makes little difference how the pattern started. The first failure may have been due to physical and psychological conditions, or even to chance; the second may come if the patient is anxiously observing himself to see if the event will happen again. After the third failure, he is convinced that something is seriously wrong. De-reflection breaks such patterns by redirecting the patient's attention away from himself and toward his partner. Impotence is likely to result in a man who observes his own sexual performance during the sex act, afraid that he will fail. And frigidity is often the outcome of a woman's anxiously watching herself in expectation of orgasm.

Psychological Hypochondriacs

De-reflection — shifting the patient's attention away from himself — is, in one sense, the opposite approach from that of orthodox psychoanalysis, which asks the patient to concentrate on himself. Freud, only two generations ago, faced a completely different situation from that facing psychiatrists today. Freud had to convince the public and the medical profession that sicknesses can be caused via the psyche in *biologically* healthy people. Frankl now has to convince the public and the medical profession that sicknesses can be caused via the noös in *psychologically and biologically* healthy people. But so successful was Freud in convincing his contemporaries that a neurosis is rooted in the psyche that many people suspect a psychological disorder when they are noölogically frustrated, or existentially empty and anxious. In addition, some people consider others sick with whom they do not get along or with whom they disagree.

In a sense, Freud himself laid the groundwork for this widespread feeling that "everyone is a little crazy," because his writings are sprinkled with statements to that effect. "Every normal person," he wrote in *Collected Papers*, "is only approximately normal; his ego resembles that of the psychotic in one point or another." Or, in *An Outline of Psychoanalysis:* "There is scarcely any condition generally recognized as normal in which it would not be possible to demonstrate neurotic traits." The theme was taken up by his leading followers, even those who modified Freud in many other ways. Erich Fromm, in *Escape from Freedom*, states that "the phenomena which we observe in the neurotic person are in principle not different from those we find in the normal." Popular conception, fed by the mass media, magnified and falsified these statements to mean that everyone had better watch himself constantly, or some hidden evil will overwhelm him. Frankl takes the example of the movie, *The Snake Pit*, to point out how the movie could start anxiety feelings in a perfectly healthy woman who, after seeing the film, may start wondering: "Didn't my mother, too, when she nursed me, let me wait, or did not my father also break my doll — did I not suffer hurts similar to those of the heroine in the movie? Of course, I do not remember — but the woman in the film did not consciously know either about these childhood incidents until analysis brought them out." And so the lady in the audience may become worried that she, too, may someday land in the snake pit of insanity. And her anxiety may start that vicious circle of fear that can become phobic. Over-attention to mental health, just as overattention to happiness or sleep, will result in the opposite of what was intended: worry about health will result in hypochondriasis, which is a sickness.

As a consequence of such misapplied logic, we now live in a society of psychological hypochondriacs in which people go through life with their ears cocked to what is going on in their own unconscious and in the unconscious of the people around them, looking for the "true" motivations of their actions, feelings, and thoughts. Readers of *Man's Search for Meaning* often express relief at the assurance that suffering, including childhood suffering, does not necessarily lead to "complexes" and neuroses. A student in Alabama wrote Frankl about her unhappy childhood — her parents were divorced and she was passed on to boarding schools and summer camps — and then commented, "I have suffered more from the thought that I should have complexes rather than from actually having them. I wouldn't trade my experiences for anything and believe a lot of good came out of them." She then wrote that she gave the book to her sister who was raised by an elderly aunt and had feelings of rejection. "She has managed to become an accomplished artist, and I feel that your book will help free her from the complexes she feels she should have — as it did me."

But many people not only succumb to the complexes they feel they "should have," considering their childhood experiences, but also observe others for the neuroses which they "ought to have." A marriage counselor said that the advice he is prompted to give most often to couples seeking his help is, "Don't analyze each other!" People are sent to psychiatrists and counselors for reasons that have little to do with mental health — children who are underperforming in school, workers who are "troublemakers," and women who have illegitimate children. Leonard J. Duhl, Director of the Professional Service Branch of the National Institute of Mental Health, declared that he was "tired of seeing so many issues being put on the shoulders of us psychiatrists. . . . They have, for example, accepted 'delinquency' as a mental health problem," which, he added, was really a social problem that should be dealt with through urban renewal, job opportunities, education, and other fields that have nothing to do with psychology.[5] One of the most outspoken critics of the everyone-runs-to-the-psychiatrist view is Thomas S. Szasz, professor of psychiatry at the State University of New York's Upstate Medical Center, who said that many patients come to psychiatrists with "mental diseases" which are really nothing but problems of living. In such cases, Szasz said, the physician has nothing to diagnose, but rather must judge whether the person is sick, or simply different, confused, difficult, or unhappy.[6]

Some psychiatrists are so indoctrinated with orthodox Freudian views that they see sickness behind any unusual behavior. A six-year-old girl suddenly refused to speak in class. The school psychiatrist, investigating her speaking, eating, and other "oral habits" became quite excited about this "unique case" and recommended analysis. The father refused because the child seemed normal in every other way. She was transferred to a different class where she spoke without trouble. It turned out that she had been shy and the teacher and some children in her original class had made fun of her, so she had withdrawn. The school psychiatrist foresaw that the "deep-seated problem," if not resolved in analysis, would emerge in other symptoms. Today, fourteen years later, the young lady is married and is a perfectly well-adjusted person.

The Limits of Debunking

The Austrian Federal Publishing Company for Education, Science, and Art in 1967 published a book, *From Freud to Frankl*, by Karl Dienelt, discussing the impact of the many European and American schools of psychiatry on mental health and education. Within the past sixty years, man's understanding of mental health has moved from the Victorian era to the space age. Freud and his disciples found it necessary to let light and fresh air into the basement of the Victorian unconscious and clear out the accumulated junk to find the treasures of truth. They pointed at the hidden, unadmitted, and often not very noble reasons that made man act the way he did, and focused on the shocking impulses that motivate his thoughts and deeds. It was healthy to release the repressed and unmask the concealed, and Gordon W. Allport gave credit to Freud for being "a specialist in precisely those motives that must not be taken at their face value." Now, sixty years later, however, the throwing out of false motives no longer is the principal problem. The problem is to keep man from throwing out, together with the falseness, the treasures of truth that Freud set out to find. Freud himself occasionally went pretty far in his debunking. In his *Collected Papers*, for instance, he defines parental love as "nothing but parental narcissism born again," and friendship as "a sublimation of homosexual attitudes." But he was also aware that the search for underlying motives can be overdone. The story is told that once, at the beginning of a lecture, he held up a cigar and admonished his audience: "Remember, a cigar may also be sometimes a cigar, and nothing but a cigar."

Frankl and his contemporaries are no longer concerned with the throwing out of Victorian face-saving masks, but with man's true face behind those masks. As Frankl put it in *Man's Search for Meaning*, "unmasking and debunking should stop as soon as one is confronted with what is authentic and genuine in man, such as his desire for a life that is as meaningful as possible. If it does not stop then, the man who does the debunking merely betrays his own will to depreciate the spiritual aspirations of another." Mental health in the space age requires a look at man as he is and as he might become in the expanding universe of human potential.

CHAPTER X

The Reality of Religion

*Two things draw me to reverence: the starry heaven above
and the moral law within.*   IMMANUEL KANT

IN PSYCHOTHERAPY, THE FIRST STEP IS to face reality. Logotherapy maintains that reality, encountered in its fullness, includes the suprahuman dimension in which ultimate meaning is located.

This may sound like a radical view for psychiatry. Freud's position on religion was most clearly expressed in a letter to his friend, Ludwig Binswanger: "I have found a place for religion, by putting it under the category of the neurosis of mankind."[1] Carl Jung, however, considered religiosity in man not a symptom of a neurosis but a possible way to a cure. Jung saw God and other religious concepts in man's unconscious in terms of archetypes. But while according to Jung man is driven by his religious instincts, according to Frankl man reaches out by his own decision. Other existential psychologists, too, see religion as the proper concern of healthy man. Abraham Maslow states, "Contemporary existential and humanistic psychologists would probably consider a person sick or abnormal in an existential way if he were *not* concerned with these religious questions."[2] Thus, psychologists since Freud have reversed themselves. Freud considered a person sick if he was religious; Maslow considers him sick if he is unconcerned with religious questions; Frankl sees man reach out for religious answers in the broadest possible sense. Preston Harold, in his latest book, *The Shining Stranger,* states, "In the development of logotherapy, Viktor Frankl has opened the psychiatrist's door not only to any one particular religion, but to religion itself. In his work one can see the dawn of a new day in psychology's history. Recognizing Freud's contributions but moving beyond them, he has transcended psychology's old 'theology' and its 'existential vacuum.' "

The Suprahuman Dimension

Man has always known — for as long, at least, as we have records of his thinking — about the existence of a dimension inaccessible to him. To have relevance, such knowledge must be personal and firsthand. Momentary and direct glimpses of life's meaning may come to anyone, but insights of great power have been attained by prophets, mystics, and artists. All important religions are originally based on their founders' direct, personal experiences with a dimension beyond man. Within limits, those experiences could be passed on to the disciples who came under the immediate influence of their masters. To be passed on further, the original experiences of the prophets had to be enshrined into sets of rules but even this indirect contact with the suprahuman through religious traditions helped believers in their search for meaning. Every religious tradition, however, eventually becomes weakened by the constantly emerging truth. Facts are discovered, new experiences contradict the original insight — or what is believed to have been the original insight — and what remains is often mostly the theoretical, unprovable, the vague, and supernatural. At this point, the religious belief becomes a set of high-sounding principles that one cannot live up to in the real world. The believers either turn away from the realities of life and concentrate on the unreal, or they come to terms with the real world drained of values and taken over by "facts." In such cases religion will support whatever is "practical," including war, tyranny, and persecution.

Eventually the time arrives when people see the original, personal experiences of the prophets as merely intellectual statements which they feel free to reject as contrary to their own experiences. In the long run, experience always wins out over intellect. When that time comes, religious tradition begins to fade, and the religious search is restored to the individual. It is a time of crisis and confusion, a period of great changes, when man finds no solution to his problems in answers learned by rote. The fundamental questions have to be asked anew, and fresh answers have to be found. Today, an increasing number of individuals feel that the exploration of the suprahuman dimension cannot be left to traditional churches, but has to become the activity of every man.

This intense and often confused exploration goes under many names ranging from religion reinterpreted to atheism. Logotherapy calls it the "search for meaning" and contributes to it a *Weltanschauung* and a terminology useful in discussing a subject for which traditional words are misleading because they have come to mean different things to different people. Logotherapy distinguishes three dimensions — the biological, the psychological, and the noölogical (or human) dimensions. The human dimension, however, enables man, at least occasionally, to touch the edges of still another, the suprahuman dimension, which contains ultimate meaning.

Actually, "touching the edge" is a misleading term. It gives the impression of a gap between the human and suprahuman dimension. But Frankl sees the higher dimension not as higher in any moralistic sense, but as "the more inclusive dimension." It includes the human dimension in the same way that man also includes the animal dimension. "Man is an animal, retains the properties of an animal, and yet is infinitely more," Frankl proposes. In this respect he compares the human dimension with a square that is part of a cube. The cube includes the square but goes an entire dimension beyond it. In the same way, the divine dimension contains the human, yet transcends it. "The human world relates to the suprahuman as the animal world relates to the human," he wrote in his compendium on logotherapy. Just as an animal cannot understand the human world from its animal dimension, man cannot understand the suprahuman and its motivations. In another one of his German books, Frankl uses the following simile: A dog will not look at a distant object to which a person's finger is pointing, but only at the finger (and will sometimes snap at it). Similarly, a man will not see what fate is pointing out, but only the finger of fate (and he, too, will sometimes rebel against his fate and snap at its finger).

This concept of man provides an intellectual understanding of the relationship between the human and the divine. But man needs more — he needs an actual experience of transcendence. This experience, having been reported by mystics since Biblical times, has become the subject of psychological research. Abraham Maslow, who has pioneered this research, reports that such "peak experiences" of awareness and participation in a higher dimension are not limited to an elect group.[2] After interviewing a great number of persons he came to the conclusion that everyone can and does have such transcendent experiences, although in some they are weaker than in others, and that some people repress them, considering them a sign of insanity or at least instability; others disregard them because such experiences do not fit their preconceived, logically built-up *Weltanschauung,* and because such people may be ultraconservative, materialistic, mechanistic, rational, or antiemotional.

These peak experiences can provide man with an element of ecstasy, a feeling of the mystery of existence, of participation in the whole, a glimpse of assurance, a fleeting awareness of a Plan of which he is a part, a meaning. One peak experience can give a man the courage to "say YES to life in spite of everything," to quote the title of another of Frankl's untranslated books. It can transfer man and his attitudes so that he sees the potentials, the opportunities, the tasks awaiting him. It can brighten the drabness and give content to the emptiness of a life, it can show a person the beauty in a pine needle, uncover the significance of a word, bring about a true encounter with a stranger (or with someone closer who until that time had been a stranger), and illuminate the true meaning of a situation. Such an experience can fuse two totally unconnected events and thoughts into a whole that makes a person momentarily aware of unknown connections everywhere, and make him see that he, too, is a vital piece in that complex jigsaw puzzle of the universe. He has to look for his own place in this puzzle, knowing that there are many other places into which he almost fits, but only one to which he really belongs.

Every living creature has this desire to be itself and have its place in the universe, but only in man is this desire conscious. The consciousness of his religious search gives man feelings of guilt, anxiety, frustration, and emptiness, but also of meaning, fulfillment, and happiness. Maslow found that these meaning-creating and blissful experiences may occur anywhere, any time, and are not limited to "holy" places and "sacred" circumstances. They produce emotional satisfaction and may even cure mental illness. He tells of two patients, one suffering from a chronic anxiety neurosis and the other from a strong obsession of suicide, each of whom was immediately and permanently cured by one peak experience. The patients *saw* meaning, experienced it firsthand, not by thinking about it or accepting someone else's experience. A peak experience is direct and personal; it is like discovering for the first time that the color "red" exists and is wonderful. "Joy exists," Maslow comments, "can be experienced and feels very good indeed, and one can always hope that it will be experienced again."[2]

Reality and Mental Health

Personal awareness of the suprahuman dimension can give the individual assurance that Order exists (even if it is not always manifest on the human level), and that he, personally, has a place in that order. The question "What is reality and what is my role?" confronts the atheist as well as the fundamentalist. Although their answers will differ, they will be based on the same assumption, namely, that there is order, participation, and relationship in the universe. For each man the world must hang together, or neurosis will result. A deep, personal conviction, even if it remains unconscious, pervades the orthodox believer, the liberal religionist, and the nonreligious scientist. It was expressed very simply by a woman in a seminar: "If faith in God gives me strength, then my God exists; he is real and near." A man, sitting next to her, who had identified himself as an atheist, agreed, "Yes, but one does not need to believe in an anthropomorphic God to have that kind of faith. One can see order in the world in humanistic terms, or in terms of ultimate meaning." Science, too, rests on the assumption that the universe hangs together. Without this faith no scientist could experiment.

Reality does not depend on man's faith, approval, or understanding. It is often glimpsed by lone individuals who disagree with majority belief. No measure of consensus makes reality true: everyone saw witches at Salem, but only one St. Paul and one Einstein had glimpses of truth. Seeing is not always believing, nor is it always a good foundation of belief. Our senses tell us that the earth stands still and railroad tracks meet in the distance. None of our senses would tell us that the tides have any connection with the moon or that matter consists mostly of empty space. Nothing in our everyday experience gives us reason to suspect that water is made of hydrogen and oxygen. Granite seems solid but it may not be any more solid than the disc created by the fast-rotating blades of an electric fan. Motion can appear as solid matter.

The reality of the human dimension can be investigated and understood by science. The reality of the suprahuman lies beyond scientific research, yet it, too, exists regardless of our understanding, or even our ability to understand. This existential interpretation of the suprahuman goes back to Biblical times when the writer of Exodus 3:14 has God describe himself as "I am that I am." Regardless of what mortals feel or speculate, reality is what it is. Reality in the human dimension has not changed from the Stone Age to the Space Age; only our understanding of it has changed. America existed before Columbus, and the earth rotated around the sun before Copernicus. Suprahuman reality, too, exists regardless of how many people believe in it, and what form their belief takes. But while our ideas about reality have no effect on reality, our growing understanding of it affects our mental health. A medieval man, believing that the earth was flat and that he literally would burn eternally for his sins, was mentally healthy. He no longer would be considered healthy today. We define as sane a person whose ideas of reality are not too far out of step with current knowledge. Considering the recent vast and rapid changes in our understanding of the physical world and religious concepts, it is not surprising that man's sanity is under more than normal strain. Man's refusal to see reality beyond the merely human dimension can result in feelings of emptiness, meaninglessness, frustration, estrangement, loneliness, anxiety, and guilt. To counter these dangers of the existential vacuum, logotherapy by no means "prescribes" religion, but simply draws attention to the fact that religion — in whatever form — cannot be excluded from the many ways in which humans have found and still can find meaning.

When the first popular article on logotherapy was published in the United States in 1954, Karl A. Menninger, educational director of the Menninger Foundation, commented: "Perhaps it is true that we psychiatrists are so afraid of endorsing religiosity and encouraging hypocrisy that we sometimes unwittingly contribute to the shyness of our patients in respect to such thoughts and communications."[3] This shyness has been confirmed by Frankl. He repeatedly found that patients who did not hesitate to discuss their sex life before a class of students became withdrawn when it came to discussing their religious beliefs. Repressed sex, thanks to Freud, has been released from many of its shackles, but repressed religiosity is on the increase.

Frankl, being no more interested in making the patient religious than Freud was in making him a sexualist, wants neither to promote nor to discourage the religious views in a patient. He has compared man's search for meaning to a train ride. Logotherapy does not provide final stations in the form of ultimate answers; it leads the patient, the religious as well as the nonreligious, to a point from which he can find his own transfers to stations beyond, to his own ultimate station. The terminal of logotherapy — meaning — lies in the direction of true religiosity. "To true religion man is not driven by the id," Frankl states, "nor should he be pressed to it by the therapist." For the doctor to give answers is not only inappropriate, it is unnecessary. Logotherapy has demonstrated repeatedly that the effect of the answer to a patient's question about his life's meaning is incomparably deeper if the answer comes from the patient, and not from the doctor.

Frankl pictures the logotherapist as furnishing the rooms of immanence without ever blocking the door that leads to transcendence: Through that door the spirit of religiosity may enter, and through it the religiosity of a person may leave. The logotherapist must not restrict the individual's choice. He must remain entirely neutral on the religious decisions of the patient. "Logotherapy," says Frankl, "simply states: man is searching. But it can never decide if he is searching for a God he has invented, for a God he has discovered, for a God he cannot find, or for himself."

Beyond the Reach of Science

Science, which was expected to disprove the existence of a divine dimension, has, on the contrary, brought into focus the limits of human reach, and therefore pointed up the existence of a dimension that lies beyond. Today, the logic of the scientists has joined the vision of the prophets in indicating the existence of a reality beyond human grasp. Scientific discovery can go only as far as the limits of the human dimension. To reach the reality that lies beyond requires a leap. Even a scientifically oriented work such as the *Encyclopedia Americana* (vol. 8, 1958) states, "How matter itself came into being is not a scientific question — its presence has to be assumed." When scientists reach the limits of the human dimension, they are faced with alternatives, none of which can be resolved on the human level. The reality of our universe is an undisputable fact, but it is based on a mystery unsolvable in the human dimension. As the astronomer George Gamov pointed out in a lecture, either there was a moment in time when something was created from nothing, or this creative moment never happened because "something" (even if only in the form of energy) always existed. Thus, the choice is between alternatives, both of which are beyond human experience: nothingness and timelessness.

The concept of time points up the difference between the human and the suprahuman dimension. On the human level, time can easily be understood: everything has a beginning and an end; our temporality begins at birth and ends with death; history is a string of events taking place in time; and we can even understand the mystery of the Now moving forever on the crest of the wave between the past, which no longer exists, and the future, which does not yet exist. But we cannot comprehend eternal time, although we know it exists beyond our comprehension. We know that time goes back before our birth, before the existence of man on earth, before the existence of the earth itself. And we also know it will go on after our death, after the end of mankind on earth, and after the end of the earth. We know that eternity exists, but it is unimaginable. Eternity is in a different dimension, where there is no past, present, nor future, no flux of time, no before and after, no beginning and end. Eternity is not a time that comes after temporal time, it is not an extension of temporal time, it is above time. It is a different concept from that of temporal time; it lies in a different dimension.

The same can be said about space. We can understand human space, but not infinity, which is not merely infinite space, beginning where finite space ends. It lies in another dimension, above finite space, although finite space is as much part of the infinite as the square is part of the cube. Eternity and infinity are incomprehensible on the human level; yet they are more than theoretical concepts. Our personal experience with our own human temporality and spatial limitations gives us some participation in the higher dimension where eternity and infinity exist. In a similar manner, we can participate in Perfect Beauty by looking for and experiencing beautiful things on the human level, partake of Absolute Truth through the millions of truths found by men, and take part in Ultimate Meaning through searching for the meanings of individual life situations. To reach Meaning, Truth, or Infinity is beyond the human dimension; we can take one step at a time in the direction of the suprahuman, but we remain limited in our human dimension.

There is evidence that science, if it cannot reach the suprahuman, can at least extend the human dimension in the direction of transcendence, and these extensions on the human level have an impact on religious belief. The great discoveries of the fifteenth century, the opening up of the globe, revolutionized man's ideas of life on earth and opened the way for the Reformation that reshaped his religious concepts. The beginning space discoveries and the opening up of the universe (even on the minute scale accessible to man) could bring a new religious reformation on a vaster scale. Space science indicates the immense gap between human and divine laws by showing that the physical laws man has experienced on earth do not necessarily apply even a short distance beyond it. The most universal earthly law, gravity, no longer holds true for the astronaut, after only a brief hop into space. Gravity, science tells us and the astronauts' experience bears this out, is far from being a universal law; it is a rare exception. It does not exist in the vast space of the universe except in those far-and-between places near stars and planets. If man is ever able to journey through space to distant stars, he will travel for years without getting close enough to those rare clumps of matter around which gravity exists. A child born in such a spaceship may well believe that the reality of gravity does not exist because it is beyond the child's experience. Man is entering a reality in which the up merges with the down, where he must orient himself by points of reference in continuous motion, and where he will have to wear magnetic shoes in order to keep his feet on the "ground." For the first time he is consciously experiencing a world of constant motion, constant change, a world of relativity in the presence of majestic order. We may be living in the beginning moments of man's spiritual space age, wherein he will need noëtic shoes of gravity to orient himself in a world without spiritual gravity. He will need a new orientation, without the familiar points of reference and without the traditional laws of nature. In such a world the survival of the fittest may no longer mean the biologically strongest or the instinctually surest, but the one strongest in the area of humanness, in his spirit or noös. Only those may be able to survive who can find the meanings of the radically changed situation, just as the mammals survived in the times of the changed physical conditions of the ice age.

If gravity is not universal, if a baby born in a spaceship can grow up with no experience of this — for earthlings — inescapable physical law, what can we say about moral laws, about ultimate meaning and purpose? Perhaps we earthlings are travelers in space for whom moral laws are beyond experience. Yet, in a different dimension, moral laws and ultimate meaning exist.

The Vanishing Point

That ultimate meaning (*logos*) resides in the divine dimension, perhaps even *is* the divine dimension, is no invention of logotherapy. It is as old as the Gospel. The Greek text of John (1:1) uses the word *"logos"* which commonly has been translated into English as "the word." Keeping the original Greek word, the passage reads: "In the beginning there was logos. Logos was with God and logos was divine." To Biblical man this was no speculation, it was existential reality. It still is. Existential theologians, such as Karl Barth and Paul Tillich, stress a theology of ultimate meaning; existential psychologists, such as Frankl and Maslow, are discovering the meaning orientation of their patients; and scientists, exploring the limits of physical discovery, are facing the problem of relevance that remains outside their own inquiry. Albert Einstein is quoted as having said, "What is the meaning of human life? To find a satisfactory answer to this question means to be religious."[4]

Is logos divine, as stated in the Bible? Today, we do not necessarily accept a statement as true because it is contained in the Gospel, but rather assume that it is contained in the Gospel because it was true for Biblical man who existentially experienced it. But relevance to man 2,000 years ago is not necessarily convincing to people today, and some twentieth-century men insist on finding out whether the ancient truths are still valid. If science has made one big contribution to the religious search, it is the questioning of basic and generally accepted assumptions, encouraging man to go beyond them and to keep looking for still more basic ones. Science has taught all fields of inquiry, including religion, that blind faith has to be restricted to axioms, and that in other areas it will hinder the personal search for reality. This has been recognized by psychologists as well as theologians. Jung said in *Memoirs, Dreams, Reflections,* "The arch sin of faith, it seems to me, was that it forestalled experience. . . . In religious matters only experience counted" (p. 92). The changed view is expressed in Cardinal Newman's definition of faith as "a presumption, not a proving," and in modern Bible translations and interpretations. Contemporary Bible scholars no longer translate the above-quoted definition of God as "I am that I am," but as "I shall be that I shall be," indicating continuous evolution even on the highest level of existence. In this era of relativity, it is conceivable that even the divine force (regarded, in the past, as the essence of the absolute) may be evolving and continuously expanding as does the physical universe itself. In this era of free search for reality, God is seen not only as the ground of our existence, but also as its goal — and not necessarily a static and absolute goal, but one expanding, coaxing, guiding, and challenging man. More than twenty years ago Frankl described God's existence as analogous to the vanishing point in a drawing: "All lines in the picture converge on it, it dominates the picture but is not really 'in' it." By applying this analogy to real life, we might also say that in wandering along the road of life we always move toward the vanishing point but can never reach it. It merely coaxes us along and expands with the horizon. We can reach only landmarks in the physical landscape, never the vanishing point itself.

In the same book, *Zeit und Verantwortung*, Frankl also uses the concept of the vanishing point to explain the relationship between meanings on the human level, and ultimate meaning on the suprahuman — that unreachable, yet always beckoning goal. He suggests that if we consistently follow those "meaning lines" of our human existence, one point ought to emerge toward which they run. Although we never can reach that point, we always must keep moving toward it. This may be the way, he speculates, in which the most important Hebrew prayer ("Our Lord is One") is to be understood in its deepest sense: "to perceive all meaning as converging into a highest Meaning which, for lack of another term, we call God, so that every truth, thought to the end, means God, and all beauty, loved to the end, sees God."

A Personal God

God as vanishing point, as the eternal Present, as an impersonal evolving force, to many people, is an interesting intellectual exercise, but of no relevance to their personal lives. It has been said that existential philosophy and psychology secularize religion. But one can also say that they, at the same time, also religionize the secular: they broaden the spectrum of personal experiences from which the individual can find meaning, and thus broaden the base of religion so that it becomes acceptable to more people.

In Biblical times, religion was all-encompassing — nothing in man's experience was outside it. Man personally experienced God in every aspect of his life — in the richness of his harvest and in famines, in the beauty of a sunset and the terror of a thunderstorm, in his dreams and visions, in the ravages by an enemy and the love of his father. God Himself was seen as the Father, strict and loving, rewarding and punishing according to laws beyond man's understanding. Man was the child, secure in his knowledge that he was important enough for God to watch over him personally and to judge every one of his actions. This feeling of being sheltered and of participating in a totality was the basis for man's mental health.

Religious traditions preserved this God concept, and for millions it continues to provide security. Others, however, have come to doubt their childhood belief in the Father and, like adolescents, are revolting against the Father image of the divine reality. But, as psychology points out, rejection of the father, or even his death, does not free the child from his reality. The child achieves freedom from its father not by running away but by understanding him. It's the truth that makes us free, and truth is evolving slowly — by religious insight, scientific investigation, and personal search.

Existential philosophy and psychology do not force man away from traditional belief, but expand his freedom of choice. The evolving truth that is making us free is also freeing us from stereotyped concepts of the divine if these concepts no longer are relevant to us. It is freeing us to postulate new religious hypotheses and to check them against personal experience. This freedom is experienced not only by people who consider themselves agnostics or atheists, but also by clergymen. Episcopalian Father Robert W. Cromey, participating in a television discussion about the currently popular question of whether "God is dead," described his reaction: "It made me feel very free. If God is dead, then I don't have to pray to Him. I have never known God to answer a prayer. We are now being pushed to see the world as it really is and to accept the responsibility for its condition."

Thus, individual freedom and personal responsibleness are playing an increasing part in man's search for ultimate

meaning. To the believers in a Father God, it is He who demands and enforces responsibility in man. Nonbelievers,
however, point to the findings of psychology that a loving as
well as a tyrannical father can enslave the child and keep it
from accepting responsibleness. But modern man, the religious as well as the nonreligious, realizes that God's glory
is not diminished by man's accepting his own responsibleness,
just as God does not need man's supplication in order to be
great. It is a human concept that taking something for yourself will make something else smaller. The absolute does not
become less when the relative grows: it is the task of the
absolute to serve as a goal to the relative. God's universal
responsibleness prods man to take on responsibleness of his
own. The religious man says, "God helps him who helps himself." An atheist, in a seminar, expressed it in his way: "Religion's function is to prompt man to be good which by nature
he isn't. Personal responsibility can take this function. If
no one watches, everything is permitted. If God doesn't watch,
our own conscience can. Personal responsibility can replace
a personal God."

Thus, the atheist says man needs a theology that replaces a
personal God with personal responsibleness. The religious
person says that man's personal responsibleness must respond
to God. The crucial question for the individual is to find
the theology, or philosophy, that possesses relevance for him,
that enables him to see his personal "meaning lines" and
follow them as well as his conscience will guide him. Perhaps
it has fallen again to the Jews to be the "chosen people"
and pioneer a new direction in religion. Their unspeak-
able suffering during the Nazi regime may have initiated
a new meaning direction in theology. Richard L. Rubenstein in *After Auschwitz* states, "No Jewish theology will
possess even a remote degree of relevance to contemporary
Jewish life if it ignores the question of God and the death
camps." There are signs that the change has affected Christian thinking, too. Examples can be found in many places; in
the tremendous response to Rolf Hochhuth's play, *The Dep-*

uty; in the official toning down by the Catholic Church, after two thousand years of massacres, of blaming the Jews for the death of Jesus; and in the Pope's recent encyclical in which he follows his general demand, "let each one examine his conscience," with specific requests of responsibleness, transferring the moral command of "loving thy neighbor" to the field of economics. One need only read the daily papers about the "experimental" ministers concerned with civil rights and the social and economic conditions of their parishioners, about the "coffeehouse priests" using folksongs and other popular music and talking to God in everyday language, to recognize the changes taking place in the Christian churches — changes toward greater human responsibleness. One is tempted to paraphrase Rubenstein's observation by stating that no Christian theology will possess relevance to contemporary Christian life if it ignores the question of God and world hunger, racial equality, and war.

Man's Relationship to the Divine

Depth psychology has shown that man may be lacking a relationship with the great unknown in his psyche, and "height" psychology, such as logotherapy, is showing that he may also lack a relationship with his goals and ideals. Man finds life meaningless if he denies or represses his relationship with Ultimate Meaning.

This is the paradox of the religious search: man has faith that a divine dimension exists, can never find out what it is like, and feels the need to find a relationship with this mystery. The religious ground, whether we call it God, Universal Order, or Ultimate Meaning, cannot crumble, give way, or end, because it is eternal and limitless. It is not under us like a safety net or above us like a protective roof, but we are part of it like a temporal cell in an eternal body. The cell cannot isolate itself on the grounds that it never saw the heart that supplies it with blood. Man's relationship with the divine is inescapable, but it is up to the individual to become aware of it on his own level of understanding. Even the atheist cannot abolish this relationship. Atheism is a belief rather than a denial.

Attention to relationships is being given on all levels — physical, human, and religious. The physicists have discovered that physical matter is based on relationships of atomic particles. Existential philosophers have drawn man's attention to the I-Thou relationship between individuals and suggested that the relevance of existence lies neither in the I nor the Thou, but in the hyphen between them. Phenomenologists maintain that man can understand human experience only by paying attention to his interrelationships with his world, and that meaning is lost when the world is broken down into elements such as subjects and objects. They describe processes taking place. A person exists in a certain position at a certain place at a certain time, and is tuned in on the world at many levels through actions, thoughts, hopes, feelings, imagination, memory, and anticipation. Thus it is only one step further for religious leaders to suggest that man is also tuned in on the universe and its guiding force (whatever its reality may be) through man's hopes, dreams, imagination, and expectations.

Biblical man did not need existential philosophers and theologians to tell him the importance of his relationship with God: he experienced it every moment of his life. It made no difference to him whether God really existed in the personal form in which man saw Him — their I-Thou relationship was real, and it still is for millions today who have never heard of Martin Buber. But an increasing number of people find that their faith in the traditionally accepted assumptions of religion has been shaken. They have developed other assumptions instead; they may believe in a practical brotherhood of man, bootstrap salvation, incarnation, an evolving God, a continuous experimenter, a coaxing goal, or meaning lines running toward a divine vanishing point. Man has developed many different beliefs but underlying them all is still belief. Religion has become as existential again as it was at the time of the Bible: not concerned with religious theories but rather with individual conscience and daily experience. Man is concerned about how to live up to his potentials, how to bear unavoidable suffering, how to live in the face of inescapable uncertainty, how to find meaning and content in his individual life. In times like the present, theoretical religious concepts such as heaven and immortality become of less relevance than the reality of the religious search.

In contrast to man's search for truth on the scientific, human level, his religious search is aimed at a goal beyond his reach and understanding. And yet it is in man's nature to pursue it; he would lose his humanness if he were to discontinue the pursuit. Religion is man's relationship with the unknowable, his dialogue with transcendence. In such a dialogue, man need not, even cannot, understand the questions clearly, yet must be ready to respond. In *Between Man and Man,* Buber said, "He who ceases to make a response, ceases to hear the Word." This, perhaps, is the meaning of the Covenant: it is man's concept that God, too, will respond if man will make his strongest possible effort, on his human level, to discover his relationship to God. Man has tried to do this in many ways, but he can see his relationship only from his own, human end, and this has resulted in suffering. Man sees God as Perfection — all-powerful, wise, and just — in short, possessing the qualities which man lacks. If God did not respond to man's prayers, man assumed the fault must be his — that he was not good enough, wise enough, patient enough, that he was lacking the qualities of perfection he attributed to God. Man punished himself for not being God, for merely being human. The social sciences have shown man a truer picture of himself, and although the true nature of God is just as hidden, man has become more realistic in his relationship with the Unknown. He has found, for instance, that it is more realistic for man to strive not toward becoming an angel, but a civilized human being who functions on all human levels and with responsibleness toward all men, and that his relationship with God (what-

ever His nature) will improve as a consequence of his more
perfect relationships with other humans. Man discovered that
to demand *the* answer will bring frustration, but the continued attempt to find *an* answer may bring fulfillment; that
final answers exist in a dimension beyond him, but that he
must be satisfied in finding the answer of the immediate situation. Man is learning to appraise his shortcomings realistically
and is beginning to realize that his great opportunity lies in
his incompleteness, his chance to change, grow, evolve, and
fulfill his potentialities. Man realizes that he is unique, not
because he was created uniquely but because each individual
is free to respond uniquely. The emphasis, in short, has
shifted from God's commands, which in their totality are unknowable to man, toward man's response to what, to the best
of his abilities, he conceives God's commands to be — and to
respond to them one at a time, in each situation of his life.
Man is becoming aware of the limitations of his freedom to
respond — biologically, psychologically, and environmentally
— and realizes that to reproach himself for failure to reach
achievements beyond his natural limitations is not religion
but masochism.

In a seminar on Yom Kippur, the Jewish Day of Atonement, a participant commented on the prayerbook phrase "To
be holy unto your God" in these words: "You may understand
by 'God' anything you wish but it will be 'your God' only if
you take the initiative to relate to Him personally, and it will
be a 'holy' relationship only if it reflects God's qualities of perfection and eternity. Being human, you cannot and should not
expect to be holy with a capital *H* or perfect with a capital *P*.
All you can do is strive toward the goal of Holiness with all
your heart, with all your soul, and with all your might. To
fall short is not a sin, nor mental sickness, but a natural consequence of your humanness. It becomes sin only if you remain
unaware of it or if you become aware of it but won't change.
Your life's task is not to be holy like God, but 'unto your
God' — you, as a human, striving toward Perfection. In this
concept, atonement or forgiveness is not an act of God but an

act by you — an act of remembering your shortcomings, bringing them up to your consciousness, examining them, and avoiding them in the future to the best of your expanding awareness. By having each year an opportunity to examine your shortcomings, you are given the opportunity to grow toward the highest holiness you are capable of achieving. Keep searching and testing your limitations."

The Proof of the Divine

In man's search for individual meaning lines, the existence of a higher dimension is always presupposed, even by atheists. What most atheists reject is not a suprahuman dimension but a traditional concept of God. Some go further and reject all nontangible reality because they cannot see it.

Such a young atheist approached Frankl in 1945, after the latter's return from the concentration camps. The young man had become disillusioned by the ravages and cruelties of war and cried out: "How can I believe in God? I cannot acknowledge that there is spirit, God, a soul. Show me a soul. I cannot see it, not even through a microscope. I see tissues of brain, but no soul." Frankl asked him what had motivated him to search for the soul, and the youth said that he was motivated by his desire to find the truth. "Is this desire of yours tangible?" Frankl asked him. "Will it be visible in a microscope?" "Of course not," the young man admitted, "because it is mental. You don't see mental things under a microscope." "Ah," said Frankl, "in other words, what you in vain were searching for in the microscope, had been a condition for your search, and presupposed all along." God, spirit, the soul, the entire suprahuman dimension must be accepted on the same level. They are presupposed. In Frankl's definition, religion is man's awareness of the suprahuman dimension, and the basic trust in ultimate meaning residing in that dimension.

Yet, the demand for "proof" persists. Such proof can come only through experiencing the things that escape logical arguments. Frankl has tried to prove the existence of the divine dimension by a phenomenological approach; that is, based on the description of actual phenomena. He starts with Pascal's famous saying, "I would not seek Thee if I had not already found Thee," expressing an emotional need in man to reach out into transcendence, a need which is ultimately unexplainable, unless an awareness of the reality of transcendence had preceded it — although on a preconscious level. Frankl then turns to the phenomena of love, pointing out that love, too, must be preceded by a lovable object.

This, Frankl concedes, is not a logical proof but a description of an emotional phenomenon. "It is no more and no less proof," he says, "than Descartes' 'I think, therefore I am.' We may say, paraphrasing Descartes, 'I love (God), therefore He is.' Just as Descartes deduces the existence of the self from the act of thinking, so we may deduce God's infinite existence from our infinite love."

Such inference of the existence of God will not come easily to people who are not ready for religious experiences, who have shut the doors on them, or who have repressed their metaphysical needs. The religious believer will not only believe in the existence of God but will also be convinced that some belief in the suprahuman is held by everybody, even if only in the subconscious. This is not so absurd a statement as it may seem at first glance. Does not everyone, for instance, believe in the Thou of another person, although this Thou, the spiritual basis of his body and psyche, remains invisible? The God of the believer is something like the primary Thou, the invisible essence behind the manifestations. Coming home to Vienna, after his experiences in the death camps, Frankl wrote: "God is the primary, the ultimate Thou to such an extent that one cannot truly speak *of* God, in the third person, but only *to* him, in the second. I cannot imagine that a man who stood in a war trench or in a death camp and spoke to God, can later stand in a lecture hall and speak of God as if this were the same one he had spoken to directly, in the trench."

To speak to God is an event that eliminates the necessity

of proof. On the other hand, it is the only possible proof of a phenomenon that exists in a dimension inaccessible to man. "Man can prove, from petrified footprints, that certain animals existed thousands of years ago," says Frankl, "but God is not a petrifact. He is not something that exists as other things exist in the human dimension." And again: "He exists in a different dimension altogether, He is the ground of existence. It may be that God 'is' not in any dimension at all — He may be the co-ordinate system itself."

To attempt to prove the existence of God as we would the existence of prehistoric animals would mean to reduce the divine to the human level. The absurdity of such reductionism is illustrated in a story of a little boy who lives in the same apartment house as Frankl. One day, Mrs. Frankl met the boy on the staircase and he told her that he had decided what he was going to be when he grew up. "I shall be," he said, "either a trapeze artist or God." The boy had disregarded the dimensional difference: he dealt with God as if being God were one vocation among other vocations.

But one need not be a child to fall into the trap of reducing God to the human dimension. On a more sophisticated level this is also done by those who expect God to answer their prayers or by those who declare that "God is dead." To expect to get a direct answer from God, Frankl declares as "magical thinking." "If you get an answer it's not from God. If you have a ship and wish to probe how deep the ocean is, you send down a wave of sound, and it is reflected. And when you get the echo, you know it comes from the bottom of the ocean. However, God is infinite depth, and if you send a question and an answer comes back, it is not from God because God is Infinity. That is why you should not be astonished that God is silent. God is not dead — He is silent."

The "Language" of Religion

One's religion is as universal as human language, yet as personal as one's mode of speech. A baby makes sounds in all languages, which eventually are narrowed down to those of his mother tongue. The feeling of universal religion is also narrowed down as a person grows up in one religious tradition. But the reality of religion can be reached through many languages. The parallel between religion and language has fascinated Frankl throughout the years. Most recently, in a lecture series at Brandeis Institute, in California, he phrased it in these words: "You can arrive at truth through each language, but you may also err and lie in each language. It's up to you rather than to the language. The same, I believe, holds for religion. This does not do away with the strength of our convictions. But it does make for humility and tolerance. You need not share the belief of someone else, but you should recognize the other person's right to have a belief of his own and to let himself be led by his own conscience and nothing else. The firmer you stand in your own creed, the more your hands will be free to reach out for others. The weaker you stand in your creed, the more you will use both hands to cling to the dogma, and you then have no hands to reach out for others."

He added that the trend of today is not away from religion but "away from those denominations which have nothing better to do, seemingly, than fight each other." Denominations, however, are as important to man's religious search as one's own language is to one's search for truth. More than twenty years ago Frankl found out that there is a parallelism between religion and language. His argument runs like this: Man can approach truth only by thinking, and he can think best in his own language. Other languages may be more expressive in their shades of meaning and diversity of words, but, generally, one's own language will be the best vehicle with which to get closer to the reality that lies behind all languages. Similarly, it is a mistake to believe that true religiosity can best be achieved by staying outside all denominations. Such a person would be like a man without a language. It is, therefore, a mistake to believe that the trend is toward universal religion, an artificially contrived general religion,

a sort of religious Esperanto. Artificial religiosity is no religiosity at all. The trend, Frankl feels, is not toward universal
religion but toward an utmost personalized religion — a religion where every person eventually will be able to find a
language of his own to communicate with God.

But, Frankl adds, even if religion should ever become
individualized to the extent that each person speaks his own
religious language, he will have to use the common symbols of
religion, just as most of the different languages use the same
alphabet. Common symbols which are shared by everyone,
despite a most personalized religiosity, will always remain in
use.

Old Truths Rediscovered

Rigid believers like to assume that all that can be said about
God has been frozen in a definite form and that nothing can
be added to it. But new information about the reality of man
and his world is being added in all fields of inquiry, and it is
unrealistic to presume that religion can be exempted. Every
generation must reexamine the view of God it inherited,
and this is particularly true of the young generation today,
entering an age when the vision of the prophet, "that the
foundations of the earth do shake," is — as Tillich observes —
becoming an actual physical possibility, and might become
historical reality. Isaiah's warning that the "earth is split in
pieces" is not merely a metaphor but hard reality. It is
physics. "That," Tillich points out, "is the religious meaning
of the age into which we have entered."[5]

It is an age of puzzling paradoxes. The protection of the
old traditions is wearing thin, and new ones have not yet developed. New information is thrown at man from all sides,
conflicting with cherished beliefs. Man is finally reaping the
full consequences of his eating from the Tree of Knowledge
and his expulsion from the Garden where all paths had been
marked and where he had been guided by his instincts to find
his way. He now lives in a world of unmarked paths where at

every crossroad he must make decisions. He has vastly increased his freedom, but the knowledge to find his way is still limited. He feels anxiety because the burden of freedom is great, and he feels guilt because in every choice he knows that he could have chosen otherwise. He feels the pull forward, toward more freedom and knowledge, but also the longing for the security of the marked paths of the dim past. This two-way pull has always torn man apart, but it has become more painful because the guidance of tradition is failing, forcing man to face the fact that a return to the Garden is, indeed, blocked. He knows that he cannot relinquish his freedom, nor unlearn his knowledge, nor can he suppress his urge to reach out, if he wants to be man. He has to accept his expulsion, not as punishment but as challenge. In Buber's words (*Way of Response*), "The flaming sword of the cherubin circling the entrance of Paradise prohibits the way back. But it also illuminates the way forward."

Logotherapy helps to illuminate the way forward, step by step, and not for mankind as a whole, but for the individual. As a therapy, it deals with the individual. It tells him that he cannot change his past, but that he is not its slave either; that he can change his present and influence his future. It tells him that he has limitations but also great freedom within these, and that the use of this freedom can make the difference between a full and an empty life; that, if not used responsibly, freedom will turn into meaningless arbitrariness. It tells him that he has choices to make, at every moment, and that he must make them in the face of constant uncertainty, that he never can wait until all answers are in. It tells him that each person is alone, yet participates in a reality that far transcends him and his understanding; that success in life does not depend on the obvious; that individual life is geared to ultimate meaning. It tells him that he can never grasp the reality of the Ultimate, whatever name is given to it, but that everything depends on how he responds to its demands.

Logotherapy assumes that ultimate meaning exists but that it is ultimately unknowable for the individual. He only can guess at it by means of his conscience, which is part of his human makeup and therefore can err. And what his best guesses will reveal is not the overall Masterplan but only the meaning of one life situation at a time. He can participate in ultimate meaning only by responding, to the best of his limited capacities, to the meaning demands of the moment. The day-by-day pursuit of meaning gives content to his life. Happiness, peace of mind, satisfaction, success, are only by-products of his pursuit of meaning.

Unfailingly, brief summaries of logotherapy, like the above, bring forth claims that none of this is new. Frankl is aware of this reaction. He recalls: "When I first lectured in the United States, people told me that what I presented was something new, at least as compared with psychoanalysis. But later, on my tours in Asia, in India and Japan, I was told the contrary. People pointed out to me that what I was saying were old truths one might find in the ancient Vedas, in Zen, or in the writings of Laotse."

He considers both these evaluations of logotherapy justified and feels complimented on both counts. "It's an honor if people regard my contributions as something new, but it is equally an honor when they see old truths in logotherapy. Karl Jaspers once remarked that in philosophy something wholly new is likely not to be fully true. That holds for psychotherapy, too. If logotherapy had achieved nothing more than to rediscover and reformulate old truths — even then it would have contributed to the advancement of psychotherapy. But I think logotherapy has taken a step further: it has made the old wisdom into a system and a method, and thus made it teachable and learnable. Seen in this light, both evaluations of logotherapy, by the Americans as well as the Asians, may be correct: the old truths had to be rediscovered and reformulated in a systematic and methodologically refined way so the individual person can apply them to his own life."

REFERENCES

BECAUSE THIS BOOK presents the world of Dr. Frankl's thoughts from many of his books, articles, and lectures, a detailed attribution to individual sources would have been distracting to the general reader for whom this volume is intended. I made a careful effort to make clear which statements and thoughts came from Dr. Frankl, and for important formulations I gave the source in the text. The interested reader is referred to the bibliography for more extensive study of Dr. Frankl's and his disciples' work.

Attributions to other authors quoted are usually made in the text. The following brief list gives the sources of some of their more important references.

Chapter I

1. Roots, John McCook, "A Human Dynamo Sparks U.S. Colleges," *Pace* (Los Angeles), May 1967.

Chapter II

1. Kline, M. Arthur, "We Are Born to Believe," *Woman's Home Companion,* April 1954.
2. "Being and Meaning," *Times Literary Supplement* (London), Oct. 29, 1964.
3. Binswanger, Ludwig, *Reminiscences of a Friendship,* New York: Grune & Stratton, 1957, p. 96.
4. Crumbaugh, J. C., and L. T. Maholick, "An Experimental

Study in Existentialism: The Psychometric Approach to Frankl's Concept of Noögenic Neurosis," *Journal of Clinical Psychology*, 1964, 20:200.

Chapter III

1. Pike, James A., "Fewer Beliefs, More Belief," *Center Diary: 14*, Center for the Study of Democratic Institutions (Santa Barbara, California), Sept.–Oct. 1966.
2. Weisskopf-Joelson, Edith, "Logotherapy and Existential Analysis," *Acta Psychotherapeutica*, 1958, 6:193–204.
3. Wertheimer, Max, "Some Problems in the Theory of Ethics," in *Documents of Gestalt Psychology*, Mary Henle, ed., Berkeley: University of California Press, 1961.

Chapter V

1. Allport, Gordon W., "Psychological Models for Guidance," *Harvard Educational Review*, 1962, 32:373.

Chapter VI

1. Maslow, Abraham, *Motivation and Personality*, New York: Harper & Bros., 1954, p. 60.
2. "Tumult and Shouting," *This World, San Francisco Chronicle*, April 30, 1967.
3. West, Louis J., "Psychiatry, Brainwashing, and the American Character," *American Journal of Psychiatry*, 1964, 120:842.
4. *Detroit News*, Feb. 20, 1963.

Chapter VII

1. Sanford, Nevitt, "Psychiatry Viewed from the Outside: The Challenge of the Next Ten Years," Symposium, *American Journal of Psychiatry*, 1966, 123(5):519–22.
2. Hutchins, Robert M., "The Issues," in *The University in America*, Center for the Study of Democratic Institutions (Santa Barbara), 1966.
3. The remarks by Clarence Faust, Walter Lippmann, and Rosemary Parks are taken from *Center Diary: 14*, Center for the Study of Democratic Institutions (Santa Barbara), 1966.

Chapter VIII

1. Committee on the College Student of the Group for the Advancement of Psychiatry, *Sex and the College Student,* New York: Atheneum, 1966.
2. Simmons, J. L., and Barry Winograd, *It's Happening,* Santa Barbara: Marc-Laird Publ., 1966.
3. "Tumult and Shouting," *This World, San Francisco Chronicle,* Sept. 18, 1966.

Chapter IX

1. Reported in the *American Journal of Psychiatry,* 1966, 123(5):519–28.
2. Boring, Edwin G., "Was This Analysis a Success?" *Journal of Abnormal and Social Psychology,* 1940, 35:4–10.
3. Allport, Gordon W., *The Individual and His Religion,* New York: The Macmillan Company, 1950, p. 92.
4. Gerz, Hans O., "Experience with the Logotherapeutic Technique of Paradoxical Intention in the Treatment of Phobic and Obsessive-Compulsive Patients," *American Journal of Psychiatry,* 1966, 123(5):548–53.
5. "The American Character," Center for the Study of Democratic Institutions (Santa Barbara), 1965.
6. Schur, Edwin M., "Psychiatrists Under Attack," *Atlantic,* July 1966.

Chapter X

1. Binswanger, Ludwig, *Reminiscences of a Friendship,* New York: Grune & Stratton, 1957, p. 96.
2. Maslow, Abraham, *Religions, Values, and Peak-Experiences,* Columbus: Ohio State University Press, 1964, pp. 18, 22, 59, 76.
3. Kline, M. Arthur, "We Are Born to Believe," *Woman's Home Companion,* April 1954.
4. Farnsworth, D. L., "The Search for Meaning," *Academic Reporter,* 5(8), Nov. 1960.
5. Tillich, Paul, *The Shaking of the Foundations,* New York: Charles Scribner's Sons, 1948, p. 3.

BIBLIOGRAPHY ON
LOGOTHERAPY

Citations preceded by an asterisk (*) served as source material for the present book.

1. Books

IN ENGLISH

*Frankl, Viktor E., *Man's Search for Meaning: An Introduction to Logotherapy,* Preface by Gordon W. Allport, Boston: Beacon Press, 1962; Paperback edition, New York: Washington Square Press, 1963.

*————, *The Doctor and the Soul: From Psychotherapy to Logotherapy* (second, expanded edition), New York: Alfred A. Knopf, Inc., 1965; Paperback edition, New York: Bantam Books, 1967.

*————, *Psychotherapy and Existentialism: Selected Papers on Logotherapy,* New York: Washington Square Press, 1967.

————, *The Existential Vacuum: A Challenge to Psychiatry* (The Dallas Lectures), New York: The New American Library, in preparation.

*Leslie, Robert C., *Jesus and Logotherapy: The Ministry of Jesus as Interpreted Through the Psychotherapy of Viktor Frankl,* New York and Nashville: Abingdon Press, 1965.

Tweedie, Donald F., *Logotherapy and the Christian Faith: An Evaluation of Frankl's Existential Approach to Psychotherapy,* Preface by Viktor E. Frankl, Grand Rapids, Mich.: Baker Book House, 1961.

————, *The Christian and the Couch: An Introduction to Christian Logotherapy,* Grand Rapids, Mich.: Baker Book House, 1963.

*Ungersma, Aaron J., *The Search for Meaning: A New Approach in Psychotherapy and Pastoral Psychology,* Philadelphia: Westminster Press, 1961.

IN GERMAN

*Dienelt, Karl, *Von Freud zu Frankl,* Wien und München: Österreichischer Bundesverlag für Unterricht, Wissenschaft und Kunst, 1967.
*Frankl, Viktor E., *. . . trotzdem Ja zum Leben sagen,* Wien: Verlag Franz Deuticke, 1946.
*———, *Zeit und Verantwortung,* Wien: Verlag Franz Deuticke, 1947.
*———, *Der unbewusste Gott,* Wien: Amandus-Verlag, 1948.
*———, *Der unbedingte Mensch,* Wien: Verlag Franz Deuticke, 1949.
*———, *Homo patiens.* Wien: Verlag Franz Deuticke, 1950.
*———, *Logos und Existenz,* Wien: Amandus-Verlag, 1951.
*———, *Die Psychotherapie im Alltag,* Wien: Verlag Franz Deuticke, 1952.
*———, *Pathologie des Zeitgeistes,* Wien: Verlag Franz Deuticke, 1955.
*———, *Das Menschenbild der Seelenheilkunde,* Stuttgart: Hippokrates-Verlag, 1959.
*———, *Die Psychotherapie in der Praxis,* Wien: Verlag Franz Deuticke, 1961.
*———, *Theorie und Therapie der Neurosen,* München: Ernst Reinhardt, 1967.

2. Chapters in Books

IN ENGLISH

Arnold, Magda B., and John A. Gasson, "Logotherapy and Existential Analysis," in *The Human Person,* New York: Ronald Press, 1954.
Frankl, Viktor E., contributions to *Critical Incidents in Psychotherapy,* ed. S. W. Standal and R. J. Corsini, Englewood Cliffs, N.J.: Prentice-Hall, 1959.
———, "Logotherapy and the Collective Neuroses," in *Progress*

in Psychotherapy, ed. J. H. Masserman and J. L. Moreno, New York: Grune & Stratton, 1959.

————, "From Psychotherapy to Logotherapy," in *Psychology*, ed. Annette Walters, Westminster, Md.: Newman Press, 1963.

————, "The Philosophical Foundations of Logotherapy," in *Phenomenology: Pure and Applied*, ed. Erwin W. Straus, Pittsburgh: Duquesne University Press, 1964.

————, "Fragments from the Logotherapeutic Treatment of Four Cases, with an Introduction and Epilogue by G. Kaczanowski," in *Modern Psychotherapeutic Practice: Innovations in Technique*, ed. Arthur Burton, Palo Alto: Science and Behavior Books, 1965.

————, "Comment on Vatican II's Pastoral Constitution on the Church in the Modern World," in *World;* Chicago: Catholic Action Federations, 1967.

Friedman, Maurice, "Viktor Frankl," in *The Worlds of Existentialism*, New York: Random House, 1964.

Patterson, C. H., in *Theories of Counseling and Psychotherapy*, New York: Harper & Row, 1966.

Strunk, Orlo, "Religious Maturity and Viktor E. Frankl," in *Mature Religion*, New York and Nashville: Abingdon Press, 1965.

Vanderveldt, James H., and Robert P. Odenwald, "Existential Analysis," in *Psychiatry and Catholicism*, New York: McGraw-Hill, 1952.

Zavalloni, Roberto, "Human Freedom and Logotherapy," in *Self-Determination*, Chicago: Forum Books, 1962.

IN GERMAN

*Frankl, Viktor E., "Grundriss der Existenzanalyse und Logotherapie," in *Handbuch der Neurosenlehre und Psychotherapie*, ed. Viktor E. Frankl, Victor E. Freiherr von Gelbsattel, and J. H. Schultz, München und Berlin: Urban & Schwarzenberg, 1959.

*————, "Wien und das Erbe Sigmund Freuds," in *Custos Quid de Nocte?* Wien: Verlag Herder, 1961.

*————, "Die Angst als Krankheitsursache," in *Die Bedrohung unserer Gesundheit*, Stuttgart: Alfred Kröner Verlag, 1956.

*————, "Die Kraft zu leben," in *Sammelband*, Gütersloh: C. Bertelsmann Verlag, 1963.

3. Articles and Miscellaneous

IN ENGLISH

Ansbacher, Rowena R., "The Third Viennese School of Psychotherapy," *Journal of Individual Psychology,* Vol. 15 (1959), 236–37.

Birnbaum, Ferdinand, "Frankl's Existential Psychology from the Viewpoint of Individual Psychology," *Journal of Individual Psychology,* Vol. 17 (1961), 162–66.

*Crumbaugh, James C., "The Application of Logotherapy," *Journal of Existentialism,* Vol. 5 (1965), 403–12.

————, "Experimental Studies in Existentialism: II. The Purpose in Life Test as a Measure of Frankl's Noögenic Neurosis" (delivered before Sec. 24 of Amer. Psychol. Assn. Annual Meeting in New York City, Sept. 1966), *Newsletter for Research in Psychotherapy* (Veterans Administration Center, Hampton, Virginia), 1966, VIII (4), 45 (Summary).

*————, and Leonard T. Maholick, "The Case for Frankl's 'Will to Meaning,'" *Journal of Existential Psychiatry,* Vol. 4 (1963), 43–48.

————, "An Experimental Study in Existentialism: The Psychometric Approach to Frankl's Concept of Noögenic Neurosis," *Journal of Clinical Psychology,* Vol. 20 (1964), 200–207.

*Fabry, Joseph, "A Most Ingenious Paradox," *The Register-Leader,* Vol. 149, No. 6 (1967), 7–8.

*———— and Max Knight (pseud. Peter Fabrizius), "Viktor Frankl's Logotherapy," *Delphian Quarterly,* Vol. 47, No. 3 (1964), 27–30.

*————, "The Use of Humor in Therapy," *Delphian Quarterly,* Vol. 48, No. 3 (1965), 22–36.

Frankl, Viktor E., "Logos and Existence in Psychotherapy," *American Journal of Psychotherapy,* Vol. 7 (1953), 8–15.

*————, "Group Psychotherapeutic Experiences in a Concentration Camp" (paper read before the Second International Congress of Psychotherapy, Leiden, The Netherlands, Sept. 8, 1951), *Group Psychotherapy,* Vol. 7 (1954), 81–90.

*————, "The Concept of Man in Psychotherapy" (paper read before the Royal Society of Medicine, Section of Psychiatry, London, England, June 15, 1954), *Pastoral Psychology,* Vol. 6 (1955), 16–26.

————, "From Psychotherapy to Logotherapy," *Pastoral Psychology*, Vol. 7 (1956), 56–60.

————, *Academy Reporter*, III, No. 5 (May 1958), 1–4.

*————, "On Logotherapy and Existential Analysis" (paper read before the Association for the Advancement of Psychoanalysis, New York, Apr. 17, 1957), *American Journal of Psychoanalysis*, Vol. 18 (1958), 28–37.

————, "The Will to Meaning," *Journal of Pastoral Care*, Vol. 12 (1958), 82–88.

————, "The Search for Meaning," *Saturday Review*, Sept. 13, 1958.

*————, "The Spiritual Dimension in Existential Analysis and Logotherapy" (paper read before the Fourth International Congress of Psychotherapy, Barcelona, Sept. 5, 1958), *Journal of Individual Psychology*, Vol. 15 (1959), 157–65.

*————, "Beyond Self-Actualization and Self-Expression" (paper read before the Conference on Existential Psychotherapy, Chicago, Dec. 13, 1959), *Journal of Existential Psychiatry*, Vol. 1 (1960), 5–20.

*————, "Paradoxical Intention: A Logotherapeutic Technique" (paper read before the American Association for the Advancement of Psychotherapy, New York, Feb. 26, 1960), *American Journal of Psychotherapy*, Vol. 14 (1960), 520–35.

*————, "Logotherapy and the Challenge of Suffering" (paper read before the American Conference on Existential Psychotherapy, New York, Feb. 27, 1960), *Review of Existential Psychology and Psychiatry*, Vol. 1 (1961), 3–7.

*————, "Religion and Existential Psychotherapy," *Gordon Review*, Vol. 6 (1961), 2–10.

*————, "Dynamics, Existence and Values," *Journal of Existential Psychiatry*, Vol. 2 (1961), 5–16.

*————, "Psychotherapy and Philosophy," *Philosophy Today*, Vol. 5 (1961), 59–64.

*————, "Basic Concepts of Logotherapy," *Journal of Existential Psychiatry*, Vol. 3 (1962), 111–18.

*————, "Psychiatry and Man's Quest for Meaning," *Journal of Religion and Health*, Vol. 1 (1962), 93–103.

————, "Logotherapy and the Challenge of Suffering," *Pastoral Psychology*, Vol. 13 (1962), 25–28.

————, "The Will to Meaning," *Living Church*, Vol. 144 (June 24, 1962), 8–14.

*————, "Angel as Much as Beast: Man Transcends Himself," *Unitarian Universalist Register-Leader*, Vol. 144 (Feb. 1963), 8–9.

*————, "Existential Dynamics and Neurotic Escapism" (paper read before the Conference on Existential Psychiatry, Toronto, May 6, 1962), *Journal of Existential Psychiatry*, Vol. 4 (1963), 27–42.

————, "Existential Escapism," *Motive*, Vol. 24 (Jan.–Feb. 1964), 11–14.

*————, "The Will to Meaning" (a section of a paper read before the Conference on Phenomenology, Lexington, Kentucky, Apr. 4, 1963), *Christian Century*, Vol. 71 (April 22, 1964), 515–17.

*————, "In Steady Search for Meaning," *Liberal Dimension*, Vol. 2, No. 2 (1964), 3–8.

*————, "The Concept of Man in Logotherapy" (175th Anniversary Lecture, Georgetown University, Washington, D.C., Feb. 27, 1964), *Journal of Existentialism*, Vol. 6 (1965), 53–58.

*————, "Logotherapy and Existential Analysis: A Review" (opening paper, Symposium on Logotherapy, Sixth International Congress of Psychotherapy, London, England, Aug. 26, 1964), *American Journal of Psychotherapy*, Vol. 20 (1966), 252–60.

*————, "Self-Transcendence as a Human Phenomenon," *Journal of Humanistic Psychology*, Vol. 6, No. 2 (Fall 1966), 97–106.

*————, "What Is Meant by Meaning?" *Journal of Existentialism*, Vol. 7, No. 25 (Fall 1966), 21–28.

*————, "Time and Responsibility," *Existential Psychiatry*, Vol. 1, No. 3 (1966), 361–66.

————, "Logotherapy and Existentialism," *Psychotherapy: Theory, Research and Practice*, Vol. 4, No. 3 (August 1967), 138–43.

Gerz, Hans O., "The Treatment of the Phobic and the Obsessive-Compulsive Patient Using Paradoxical Intention sec. Viktor E. Frankl," *Journal of Neuropsychiatry*, Vol. 3, No. 6 (July–Aug. 1962), 375–87.

*————, "Experience with the Logotherapeutic Technique of Paradoxical Intention in the Treatment of Phobic and Obses-

sive-Compulsive Patients" (paper read at the Symposium of Logotherapy at the Sixth International Congress of Psychotherapy, London, England, August 1964), *The American Journal of Psychiatry*, Vol. 123, No. 5 (Nov. 1966), 548–53.

———, "Reply," *American Journal of Psychiatry*, Vol. 123, No. 10 (April 1967), 1306.

Grollman, Earl A., "Viktor E. Frankl: A Bridge Between Psychiatry and Religion," *Conservative Judaism*, Vol. 19, No. 1 (Fall 1964), 19–23.

———, "The Logotherapy of Viktor Frankl," *Judaism*, Vol. 14 (1965), 22–38.

Harrington, Donald Szantho, "The View from the Existential Vacuum," *Academy Reporter*, Vol. 9, No. 9 (Dec. 1964), 1–4.

Haworth, D. Swan, "Viktor Frankl," *Judaism*, Vol. 14 (1965), 351–52.

Johnson, Paul E., "Logotherapy: A Corrective for Determinism," *Christian Advocate*, Vol. 5 (Nov. 23, 1961), 12–13.

Jones, Elbert Whaley, "Nietzsche and Existential-Analysis." A dissertation in the Department of Philosophy submitted to the faculty of the Graduate School of Arts and Science in partial fulfillment of the requirements for the degree of Master of Arts at New York University 1967.

Kaczanowski, Godfryd, "Frankl's Logotherapy," *The American Journal of Psychiatry*, Vol. 117 (1960), 563.

———, "Logotherapy — A New Psychotherapeutic Tool," *Psychosomatics*, Vol. 8 (May–June 1967), 158–61.

Leslie, Robert C., "Viktor E. Frankl's New Concept of Man," *Motive*, Vol. 22 (1962), 16–19.

Maholick, Leonard T., ". . . to Comfort Always," *Journal of the Medical Association of Georgia*, Vol. 50 (1961), 559–60.

Maslow, A. H., "Comments on Dr. Frankl's Paper," *Journal of Humanistic Psychology*, VI (1966), 107–12.

Müller-Hegemann, D., "Methodological Approaches in Psychotherapy: Current Concepts in East Germany," *American Journal of Psychotherapy*, Vol. 17 (1963), 554–68.

Pervin, Lawrence A., "Existentialism, Psychology, and Psychotherapy," *American Psychologist*, Vol. 15 (1960), 305–309.

Polak, Paul, "Frankl's Existential Analysis," *American Journal of Psychotherapy*, Vol. 3 (1949), 517–22.

Rowland, Stanley J., Jr., "Viktor Frankl and the Will to Meaning," *Christian Century*, Vol. 79 (June 6, 1962), 722–24.

Schachter, Stanley J., "Bettelheim and Frankl: Contradicting Views of the Holocaust," *Reconstructionist*, Vol. 26, No. 20 (Feb. 10, 1961), 6–11.

"That Nothing Feeling," *Time* Magazine (June 1, 1962), 48.

"The Doctor and the Soul. Dr. Viktor Frankl," *Harvard Medical Bulletin*, Vol. 36, No. 1 (Fall 1961), 8.

"The Father of Logotherapy," *Existential Psychiatry*, Vol. 1 (1967), 439.

"Viktor Frankl," *The Colby Alumnus*, Vol. 51 (Spring 1962), 5.

Weiss, M. David, "Frankl's Approach to the Mentally Ill," *Association of Mental Hospital Chaplains' Newsletter* (Fall 1962), 39–42.

Weisskopf-Joelson, Edith, "Some Comments on a Viennese School of Psychiatry," *Journal of Abnormal and Social Psychology*, Vol. 51 (1955), 701–703.

———, "Logotherapy and Existential Analysis," *Acta Psychotherapeutica*, Vol. 6 (1958), 193–204.

———, "Paranoia and the Will-to-Meaning," *Existential Psychiatry*, Vol. 1 (1966), 316–20.

Wirth, Arthur G., "A Search for Meaning," *Improving College and University Teaching*, 1961, 155–59.

4. Films, Records, and Tapes

Frankl, Viktor E., "Logotherapy," a film produced by the Department of Psychiatry, Neurology, and Behavioral Sciences, University of Oklahoma Medical School.

——— and Huston Smith, "Value Dimensions in Teaching," a color television film produced by Hollywood Animators, Inc., for the California Junior College Association. Rental or purchase through Dr. Rex Wignall, Director, Chaffey College, Alta Loma, California.

———, Three Lectures on Logotherapy, given at the Brandeis Institute, Brandeis, California 93064. Long-playing records.

———, "Man in Search of Meaning" and "Youth in Search of Meaning," tapes produced by Sound Seminars, Recorded Lectures for Colleges and Universities, 3402 Clifton Avenue, Cincinnati, Ohio 45220.

INDEX